INTERPET
HANDBOOKS

CREATING A
NATURAL
AQUARIUM

INTERPET
HANDBOOKS

CREATING A
NATURAL
AQUARIUM

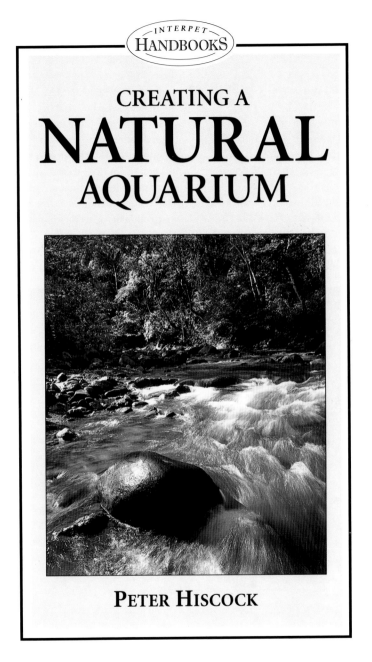

PETER HISCOCK

Howell Book House

© 2000 Howell Book House
An Imprint of IDG Books Worldwide, Inc.
An International Data Group Company
909 Third Avenue
New York, NY 10022
ISBN: 0-7645-6141-3

Credits
Created and designed: Ideas into Print,
New Ash Green, Kent DA3 8JD, UK.
Computer graphics: Stuart Watkinson.
Photo location: The Water Zoo.
Production management: Consortium,
Poslingford, Suffolk CO10 8RA, UK.
Print production: Sino Publishing
House Ltd., Hong Kong.
Printed and bound in China.

The author
Inspired and encouraged by his parents,
both accomplished marine biologists,
Peter Hiscock began keeping fish and
aquariums as a child. He was appointed
manager of a retail aquatics outlet at just
17 years of age and went on to complete
aquatic studies at Sparsholt College in
Hampshire, UK. He entered publishing
with contributions to the aquatic press.
His main interests include fish behaviour
and the interaction of fish with their
environment, as well as aquascaping and
the natural habitats of aquarium species.

Below: A shoal of rummy-nose tetras.

Contents

Introduction 10

The path of a river 12-17

Making a biotope aquarium 18-23

Aquascaping 24-39

A mountain stream 40-47

A Central American stream 48-55

A Central American river 56-63

An Australian river 64-71

A European river 72-79

A flooded forest 80-87

An Amazon acid pool 88-95

A Southeast Asian swamp 96-103

Lake Malawi 104-111

A darkened cave 112-119

A brackish estuary 120-127

A mangrove swamp 128-135

Index and credits 136

Note: Throughout this book, capacities are quoted in litres. To convert litres to imperial gallons, multiply the number by 0.22. To convert litres to US gallons, multiply the number by 0.26.

Reflections of nature

In nature, fish can be found in virtually every water system. The tropical freshwater fish commonly found in the hobby are from a wide variety of areas spanning the entire globe. In all these areas there are various habitats that are unique in style, giving us endless scope for recreating natural aquascapes. In fact in some areas, completely different habitats can be found within a few kilometres of each other. Habitats can also change dramatically throughout the year. As the seasons affect the environment of the fish, the whole style of life for living organisms in the area can change. Freshwater fish come from many river and lake systems where the water quality may vary dramatically throughout the year or even in one day. Tropical freshwater fish have evolved to cope with such changes, which makes them ideal for aquariums. It does not mean that they will tolerate bad conditions, just that they have a better capacity to cope with change.

Recreating natural aquascapes can add a whole new dimension to the hobby. A well-aquascaped natural aquarium is the closest we will get to nature in our own living rooms and the fish will appreciate it, too. A biotope aquarium is one where the decor and livestock are matched to a natural biotope, or habitat, in nature. A Lake Malawi aquarium may mimic the rocky landscape of the lake or an Amazon acid pool aquarium may be full of wood debris with dark, stained water. By trying to recreate the natural home of the fish we keep we are creating a scene within the aquarium and allowing the fish to act as they would in the wild. You could say that the aquarium becomes a stage and the fish the players on it.

THE PATH OF A RIVER

If you look at a river from its source to its end you will see a variety of ecosystems, each with its own habitats. Most tropical freshwater fish are from river systems; by their shape and behaviour you can tell which part they are from.

In the beginning

From the ground, melting snow, or rain, water collects to form small clearwater streams. This is the start of the river's long journey.

The river begins in the hills, with run-off from the ground, water from springs beneath the rocks or melt-water from snow and ice. The water from rain and snow is obviously clear, but so is water from the ground and rocks, because it has been through a natural filtration process. The water collects in small tunnels and streams that combine to form larger streams and, eventually, a small river. This is fast-flowing over rocks and waterfalls. The water is clear and fresh and has a low organic load. Many of the animals living in its waters feed off the simplest living organisms; algae and small filter-feeders such as daphnia form the diet of some larger animals in these areas.

Raging river
As the small river picks up water from contributing streams, it becomes larger, faster and more

Right: Once the streams have joined and the land becomes flat, the river begins to calm and widen. This stretch of river in Belize is surrounded by tropical rainforest that will add organic material to its waters.

violent. A few large waterfalls tumble down this steep section of the river course and it flows over bedrock and boulders smoothed by the erosion from particles in the constant torrent of moving water.

Many algae-eaters, such as the whiptail catfish and plecostomus species, enjoy these conditions. Their specially designed mouths have two main functions: removing tough algae for food and holding on to rocks and wood against the swift current. Their streamlined bodies and powerful caudal (tail) fins allow these fish to move quickly in short bursts against the current of the river.

Other fish, such as the White Cloud Mountain minnow and the danio family, are also designed to live in these fast-flowing waters. These small, torpedo-shaped fish dart through the river at speed and hide in nooks and crevices with little water movement to rest and recuperate before darting off again to search for small bugs.

Life in the forest

As the hills or mountains level out, the river begins to calm down and take a winding route over the undulating landscape. It widens and may pass through dense forest areas. Nearby pools, formed by floods or leftover pieces of a previous river route, may contain isolated populations of fish and other aquatic animals.

The riverbed is now a mixture of large gravel and sediment, picked up from the surrounding land and from its journey down the mountains. Further down the river there are sandbanks on the inside of bends, and on the other side, exposed tree roots and overhanging banks offer protection for smaller fish. Larger predatory fish live in the open waters, cruising around for a meal or resting camouflaged, just waiting for a meal to arrive by itself.

Overhanging vegetation provides rich pickings for aquatic life in the form of insects, grubs and fruits. Due

From the mountains to the sea

Many rivers start in the mountains. As rain falls, tiny streams form and join together.

Here the vegetation is heavy. In tropical environments, rainforests form and life in the river changes. Fruits and seeds, plus animal and plant waste offer plentiful food for the fish.

The main body of the river is formed as the streams join. In this area the river is still a rocky and barren environment, interspersed with waterfalls and rapids.

Emerging from the forest, the river takes with it organic matter that alters the water chemistry. Now it is soft, slightly acidic and may be muddy or brown.

to an increase in organic matter, the water quality changes slightly and becomes more acidic, with a hint of yellow-brown coloration.

Two rivers are better than one

Heading towards the oceans, many rivers join together into one gigantic mass of water, occasionally measuring many kilometres across, as in the Amazon. Where rivers join, there is a great turbulence of water. Rivers have individual water conditions and it may be a great distance before two rivers are truly

Right: Here the warmer, dark waters of the River Negro join the Amazon at Manaus in Brazil. These rivers have entirely different water qualities and do not mix for a considerable distance.

mixed into one. Viewed from the air, there is a clear definition for some distance when a muddy river carrying a mass of silt joins a clearer main river.

In this wide expanse you find some larger fish, including predatory catfish such as the redtailed cats and other much larger species. By this stage the river will have picked up a mass of sediments, rocks and organic debris and is ready to dump them into the ocean.

The joining of two rivers causes a great disturbance this far downstream. Often, the quality of the water in one river is very different to the other and it may be some distance before the two are truly mixed into one.

Add a pinch of salt

Eventually, the river must come to an end and heading downhill, its last port of call is the wide expanse of the oceans. But this end is not a sudden one; it is a long process that can continue for hundreds of kilometres. The river will widen as it joins the sea and flows with the tides.

At first, the less dense fresh water floats on top of the sea water, but eventually they mix to become brackish, the salinity varying with the tides. When the tide is out, the river will occupy a very small area of the carved-out river basin and flows directly into the sea. As the tide comes in, it will follow the river basin upstream and the waters will mix, becoming brackish. At high tides, parts of the river that usually contain only fresh water will be

Finally the river meets the ocean. Spreading out over a wide expanse, the river is now heavily laden with sediment. Salt water moves up and down the final run of the river, creating an ever-changing estuarine habitat.

Now the river is a great mass of water. The soil here is easily carved by the river as it winds back and forth across the land. As it turns, the water moving on the outside of the bend is faster and carves away at the land. On the inside bend, sediment is deposited, creating sandy banks.

pushed back by oncoming sea water. This area of the river is called an estuary and relatively few fish thrive in these conditions. Most freshwater fish will tolerate a small amount of salt, but comparatively few accept brackish conditions. With salinity altering daily with the tides, fish either have to learn to cope or constantly swim with the tide, travelling many kilometres up- and downstream every day.

In some brackish areas, you find fish such as archerfish. They 'spit' mouthfuls of water at insects above the surface, causing them to fall into the water and become the next meal. Mangrove swamps develop in some large rivers. In these areas, the water is calm and salty, but the mangrove trees have adapted to live happily with their roots in these conditions. The roots provide a superb habitat for many tropical fish that use them for protection and cover.

In sandy tropical estuaries you find mudskippers out of the water resting in the mud. Their specially developed eyes allow them to see both in and out of water. Brackish water fish show just how nature and evolution will find a way to inhabit every possible area.

Life in the lakes
Of course, rivers are only one place where fish can be found. There are a number of lakes and pools where fish live, often completely isolated from rivers. Some freshwater lakes in North America, Africa and Asia are so vast that they look like oceans. Their gigantic size means that some

lakes are even affected by the pull of the moon, creating small tides.

The most common 'lake-only' fish kept in the hobby are those from the African Rift Valley lakes of Victoria, Tanganyika and Malawi, the most popular being the Malawi cichlids. In this environment, hundreds of fish are grouped in small areas around rocky outcrops near the shore. In fact, you will find most fish in the sunlit shallows, because there is not much in the lake for them to eat other than 'aufwuchs', a collective name for the algae and small creatures that live amongst it.

Acid water
Some lakes in tropical forest regions are the result of a previous annual river flooding. Lakes may be permanent, but many dry up within a few months. In this environment the water becomes very acid, due to a buildup of organic debris from the surrounding vegetation. Lakes can reach a pH level as low as 5.0 before the fish start to die. Many tetras and other Amazonian species prefer slightly acid water and will be happy at a pH of between 6.5 and 7.0.

Some of these pools are large enough to support a thriving community of fish until the next flood, when the pool is refilled with water from the river. Many fish use this period of flooding to breed. The larger mass of water and new hiding areas amongst forest vegetation means there is less chance of meeting predators, and the influx of washed-up creatures, insects and fruits ensures that food is plentiful.

Pleasure pools

In some areas of Africa, a group of fish called killifish live in small pools that rapidly dry up when the rains stop. The fish live off insects and bugs that stray into the pools and puddles. The fish survive these extreme conditions by breeding rapidly and laying eggs in the mud before the pool dries up. The parents die, but their eggs are left dried and dormant beneath the now hard mud. When the rains come again, the eggs are reanimated and will hatch, so that the cycle starts again.

Some of these fish have a natural lifespan of just a few months, but in the aquarium, many killifish will live

Below: This river in the Philippines has reached the end of its journey as it mixes with sea water to create a brackish environment studded with mangroves.

for years and attain sizes much larger than they would in the wild.

Swamp creatures

In contrast to the drying pools of Africa, many fish live in permanent, heavily vegetated bodies of water. The swamps of Malaysia and Borneo are home to many loaches and to the large group of labyrinth fish. They are so-called because of the labyrinth organ, a form of 'lung' that only they possess. This evolutionary development allows the fish to obtain oxygen from atmospheric air. This is extremely useful, as the swamps often become stagnant and starved of oxygen.

The low oxygen and high organic levels in the area are a boost for aquatic plants that become so densely packed that the flow of water is reduced to virtually nothing.

MAKING A BIOTOPE AQUARIUM

A biotope aquarium brings not only the fish into your home, but a whole aquatic environment. In familiar surroundings, fish will behave as they would in nature and supply the viewer with a source of endless fascination.

Quite at home

This bulldog catfish, *Chaetostoma* sp., is quite at home resting on a piece of wood and may actually need bogwood as a vital part of its diet.

There are two ways to go about creating a biotope aquarium. The first may be the correct way, but is by far the hardest and most limiting. This method is to select only the fish and plant species that are seen in the area you are trying to recreate and to use only the correct rocks and decor to reproduce accurately the natural habitat. The second option – and the one adopted here – is to represent (not reproduce) the natural habitat in the aquarium. Plant species need not be accurate, just representative of the kind of foliage in the area. Generally speaking, the fish species you include should only be fish from the area, but there are no strict rules; you can include other species, providing they fit in well with the other inhabitants. Remember that the aim is to create an exciting, lively display and if you try to be totally realistic, the results may be disappointing. The natural biotope is a template to work around, not a precise specification to be followed. Imagine we were to create a biotope aquarium of a brackish estuary. If we did this exactly, we would have a bare aquarium full of mud with a rock in the middle. This is what a one-metre stretch of many estuaries looks like. However, throughout the estuary you can find other objects, such as driftwood, branches and rocks, as well as one or two plants. If we include all of this in the aquarium we have a much better display, while still representing the natural habitat.

Non-biotope aquariums

Of course, a natural aquarium does not have to represent a biotope. A natural aquarium can be defined as one in which the decor is not only ideally suited to the fishes' needs, but also aesthetically pleasing to the viewer. It is essential to include only materials found in nature, although some of the very realistic 'fake' rocks and roots available would be quite acceptable in a natural aquarium. However, fluorescent air-powered ornaments would look out of place.

Just add fish

Getting the plants and decor right will create the picture, but it is the fish that will bring it to life. The aquarium you construct will be a

Below: In nature, there is a vast array of habitats and environments. To recreate this forest pool in an aquarium, use the correct decor and water parameters.

home for your fish and should be tailored to their requirements.

It is very important to find out as much as you can about the fish you plan to keep. Research their breeding habitats and offer an environment suitable for breeding. Create plenty of hiding places. Remember that fish from the same area in the wild will not necessarily coexist peacefully in an aquarium; they may be predator and prey, territorial or simply exhibit a clash of personalities.

Try to recreate the fish's life in nature as accurately as possible. Examine its habits, find out what it feeds on and where it spends most of its time. Shoaling fish, such as most tetras, should be kept in groups in the aquarium. This way they will feel more comfortable and confident, they will be healthier and show brighter colours. Many gouramis come from swamps with dense vegetation and very slow water movement. These fish would not appreciate fast water movement, so reduce the flow on the filters or disperse water using spray bars.

All this planning and research helps to contribute to the creation of a natural aquarium, one where the decor, the equipment and the inhabitants all combine perfectly.

Equipment – the bare minimum

The first thing you will need is an aquarium. The standard glass box is fine, but today there are many designs to choose from, some better than others. It is possible to have almost any size aquarium designed at a reasonable cost. Cabinets and hoods are also available in a wide range of shapes, sizes and colours.

A tank measuring 90x30x45cm (36x12x18in) was used to create all the biotopes featured in this book.

*Using different filter
media in an external
power filter gives you
more control over
water parameters.*

The design of
aquarium can be
directly related to the
style in which you
decorate it. For
example, if you plan to
create a fast-flowing
river setup, you may
wish to use a long narrow
aquarium to enhance the
effect of movement and to
'channel' the water visually.
Alternatively, a Lake Malawi setup
may need to be deeper and wider
than normal to accommodate a
'wall' of rockwork.

The new rectangle
Manufacturers are now creating
hexagonal aquariums, bow-fronted
aquariums, round aquariums,
octagonal aquariums, aquariums
with sloping fronts and even
aquariums joined together by tubes.
It is important to be aware of the
difference between innovation and
gimmickry. Angled aquariums can
distort the image of the fish as they
swim past the many corners. This
makes hexagonal and octagonal
aquariums effective only when they
are very large. Plastic hexagonal
'twin' aquariums joined together by
tubes are simply gimmicks that treat
the inhabitants as if they were
domestic hamsters. And an aquarium

in which you cannot
easily house a suitable filter
is not good enough for *any*
fish to live in.

The all-in-one setup
One of the best choices
for a new aquarium is the
all-in-one setup. These
are very good value
because they contain all
the equipment you need
for the specific aquarium.
This means that you will
have the correct size heater,
filter and correct lighting all
built into the aquarium.
Often, the heating and filtration
are combined in one tidy black box.
The only problems with the all-in-
one solution occur when you decide
to start changing things. For some
biotope designs, you may need to use
external filtration, faster or slower
flow rates or specially designed
lighting. These are hard to alter
when all the items are fixed in place.

Life support
Of all the equipment needed,
filtration is the most vital. It is the
life-support system for your fish;
without a form of filtration they will
die. In nature, large volumes of water
will dilute waste and bacteria will
remove it. In the aquarium, the
volume of water is greatly reduced,
so the number of bacteria have to be
increased far beyond natural levels.
This is the job of filtration.
The two most common forms of
filtration are supplied by internal and
external power filters. Undergravel

21

filters are still readily available but have been superseded by the power filters. Although some people favour undergravel filtration, it presents major problems for aquascaping. Undergravel filtration limits the types of substrate you can use, large rocks create 'dead spots' in the filtration and the water movement undermines the plants.

Internal power filters are effective and can be hidden behind rocks or wood, but by far the best filter for use with aquascaping is the external power filter. This sits outside the aquarium and the only parts hidden in the tank are the inlet and outlet tubes. Using external filters allows you to control the flow rate inside the aquarium more easily, using spray bars and diffusers. The filters can also be cleaned and maintained without fuss outside the aquarium.

Heating

Today there is virtually only one practical form of maintaining heat within a domestic aquarium and that is with the commonly available heater/thermostats. These are very accurate and easy to hide within the aquarium. Be sure to position them near a flow of water so that the heat is evenly dispersed. It is possible to buy combined heater/thermostats and external filters. These are ideal for aquascaping, because they leave no visible equipment inside the tank.

If you plan to use large rocks or large fish in your display, it may be worth investing in a heater guard. This small device is simply a sturdy plastic mesh that protects the heater/thermostat from falling rock-work and aggressive or jumpy fish.

Lighting

Most standard aquariums use fluorescent tube lighting, which is widely available. Use only aquatic lighting tubes; domestic lights are unsuitable and potentially dangerous and you will be unable to achieve the correct spectrum of light to grow plants or enhance fishes' colours.

Aquatic fluorescent tubes are designed with a specific purpose. Some promote plant growth, others

Aquarium heater/thermostats can be set to the desired temperature for your fish and are very accurate. Only use them underwater, where they will switch themselves on and off as required.

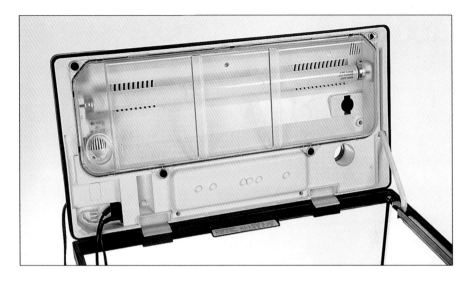

Above: This fluorescent light tube is built into the aquarium hood and protected from any condensation or splashing by a plastic cover. Waterproof fittings are also available for fluorescent aquarium lights.

will bring out the colours of the fish. It is possible to combine different tubes to achieve certain effects.

If you are planning to use plants quite heavily, you might consider investing in a metal halide or mercury vapour lamp. These lamps have a very intense bright light that can penetrate deeper water with ease. If this option is too costly, then add more fluorescent tubes.

Spotlights can really add to the mood of a well aquascaped tank. Highlighting gaps in plant growth or just catching the edges of

rocks and wood can look highly impressive. This type of lighting will simulate the effect of shafts of sunlight penetrating the overhanging vegetation.

Underwater lighting is also available for the aquarium. Although it can be hard to use to natural effect, it can make a real difference if it is powerful enough. Highlighting areas from underneath or from behind a rock creates an atmosphere of mystery and draws attention to otherwise hidden areas. Underwater lighting will work best in a dimly lit aquarium or one furnished with plenty of floating plants to block out the light from above.

Although relatively expensive, this mercury vapour lamp is very bright and ideal for plant growth.

23

AQUASCAPING

Make sure that the materials you choose will look good together and will suit the biotope or style you have in mind for your aquarium. Avoid mixing too many types of rock or wood; keeping things simple often gives the best results.

There are many materials available to aquarists, but it is important to understand the role they play and how they work, as many are only suitable for specific fish. Some rocks will alter the chemistry of the water, making it hard, alkaline and uninviting to many fish. A few materials can do the opposite and create soft, acid conditions.

Gravel

There are several types of substrate available, the most common one being pea gravel, so called because it

Preparing the ground

The foundation of the construction – the substrate – will act as a planting medium and a support for the weight of rocks and wood.

is small and rounded. It is usually sold in a range of sizes or grades. Pea gravel is an all-purpose medium and does nothing particularly impressive on its own. Some pea gravel will contain lime, which can raise hardness and pH, so check before you buy. However, the quantities usually found in this gravel will not

Grades of aquarium gravel

Use coarse gravel over sand for stream bed displays.

Medium gravel is a good all-round substrate for many aquarium setups.

have a major effect on water quality.

Lime-free gravel is also available. This is often a fine-graded gravel and golden-brown in appearance. It is an excellent medium for planting, and small and light enough for bottom-dwelling fish to sift around in.

Larger gravels over 1cm (0.4in) in size are not suitable for plant growth and can trap large organic particles. Avoid these or use them together with smaller grades. If you wish to use large gravel, place a layer of it on top of a smaller substrate.

To achieve a special effect, you can find alternative and unusual gravel substrates that vary in texture and colour. Larger garden centres are often a good source for unusual substrates, but try to find out what rock the gravel is made from and whether it will alter water chemistry before using them.

Fine gravel provides a good substrate for plants.

Sand
Of course, gravel is not the only substrate available. Sand has recently become popular in home aquariums. If you choose sand, buy it from aquatic stores or look for 'silver sand', which will not alter the water chemistry. Sand is an excellent medium for plants to root in and good for rocks to rest on. However, it does have its drawbacks. Firstly, it will easily compact and create areas of no oxygen that turn black and noxious. To avoid this happening, stir it regularly to stop any compacting. Secondly, fish find it very easy to move around and larger fish can quickly ruin a display and clog filters by wafting sand into suspension. And finally, mulm and organic debris will also collect on the surface of a sand substrate, but this is easy to remove with a siphon. Some people like the aquarium to be clean, neat and tidy all the time, but a bit of muck and mulm on the

Sand and fine gravel

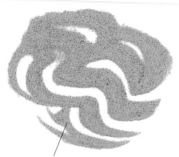

Fine sand provides a good foundation for rocks.

Lime-free fine gravel will not affect water chemistry.

substrate and a slight untidiness add to the natural look of the display.

Of course, mixing substrates is possible and can often be used to good effect. Coloured gravel is usually rather garish, but black gravel mixed with other substrates, such as standard pea gravel, darken the overall look and help to create a moody atmosphere. Other dark substrates include basalt chips or even crushed coal. All these substrates can help to show up the colours of some of the fish.

So far, we have avoided any substrates that alter the water chemistry, but some are designed to do just that. Coral gravel or coral sand, which are normally found in the marine aquarium, can be used in freshwater aquariums where the inhabitants, such as some of the African lake cichlids, prefer high pH and hardness levels. This fine white gravel is made from crushed shells and coral as you would often see on a shoreline and is full of minerals such as calcium carbonate. The calcium is released into the water naturally until it reaches a certain hardness. At this point the coral will 'buffer' the pH and hardness and keep the levels constantly high.

Calcareous substrates

Use calcareous gravel to raise pH levels in the aquarium.

Coral sand will also raise pH levels.

Planting substrates

If you intend to plant your aquarium quite heavily, it is worth paying due attention to the substrate and how the plants use it. As we have seen, sand and fine-grade, lime-free gravel are good for plants, which plough their roots into a very fine substrate to become established. They must also extract nutrients from the substrate. A fine-grade material provides more surfaces for bacterial growth and the breakdown of organic matter to release nutrients.

One good way of giving the plants what they need is to add a thin layer of nutrient-rich planting substrate between two layers of sand or very fine substrate. Specially designed substrates full of nutrients are available in most aquatic outlets and really do give the plants a boost. Always buy a recommended brand; this is one product that can be quite expensive, but good brands will last for up to three years before they begin to lose nutritional values.

The nutrient-rich layer should be 'sandwiched' for two reasons. The first is simply to make sure that the plant roots can find it. If it is too deep, some roots may not reach it. If it is too high, it will be moved around by fish on the surface. The second reason is that many planting substrates float and most will very quickly make the water dirty if they are disturbed.

Another thing that plant roots love is heat. As the result of various natural processes, the substrate is often warmer a few centimetres down than the ambient water temperature. This heat in the substrate creates convection currents that help to release and move nutrients around the substrate so that they are readily distributed and available to plant roots. This liking for heat in the substrate is one reason why plants will not do well with undergravel filtration. Undergravel filters constantly circulate water from the aquarium through the substrate,

Right: Combining different substrates can be beneficial to plant growth. Here, a nutrient-rich substrate is sandwiched between two other substrates. If you combine this planting strategy with a specially designed heating cable, your plants will thrive.

which not only removes the available nutrients, but also passes cooler water over the roots.

The higher temperature around the roots and the nutrient-carrying convection currents can be recreated within the aquarium with the help of heating cables designed to be buried beneath the substrate. These cables are usually low-wattage, so they can be left on continuously without affecting the water temperature. Surround the cables with about 5cm (2in) of sand to distribute the heat evenly, followed by a thin layer of nutrient-rich substrate and another 5cm (2in) layer of sand or fine-grade, lime-free gravel. Top this off with any other kind of substrate you choose. Your plants will positively thrive in this kind of environment.

Which rocks to use

Inert rocks that are safe to use in the aquarium
Basalt, coal, flint, granite, lava, quartz, sandstone, slate.
Note: Lava rock is only suitable once it has been weathered and cleaned. When fresh, it is quite poisonous. Be sure to obtain lava rock from an aquatic retailer.

Rocks that will alter the water chemistry
Chalk, limestone, marble, tufa.
As with most substrates, be sure to wash all rocks thoroughly before placing them in the tank.

Rock 'n' roll

Rocks suitable for the aquarium can range from smooth, rounded cobbles to jagged stones and brittle slate. In aquascaping, rocks can be a very powerful tool. Positioned with care, a single large rock that may look incredibly boring on its own can become the centrepiece of a display. Densely planted aquariums can benefit from a couple of large rocks to break up the display without leaving an empty space, and just imagine how a mountain stream would look without any rocks in it.

While substrates affect the water quality to varying degrees, rocks tend to be either completely inert (they will not react with anything) or they raise pH and hardness in a similar way to coral gravel. Luckily, there is an easy test to determine whether a rock is inert or not. Anything that is likely to raise pH and hardness must be alkaline in nature and have a degree of solubility. This means that it will quite easily react with a fairly weak acid. To test this, place a few drops of normal vinegar onto a rock. If it reacts, it will gently fizz and bubble; if not, then your rock is inert and safe to use in the aquarium.

When using rocks or any large heavy objects, it is important to remember that you are dealing with a glass aquarium. Any falling rocks could be disastrous, so make sure they are stable in the aquarium. If

Aquarium bogwood

This bogwood has been cleaned and prepared for aquarium use.

You may need to clean and soak bogwood before use. This type may be called many different names, such as 'Jati wood'.

you do stack them, make sure they cannot easily fall or be pushed over. Protect heater/thermostats as well; keep them above the rockwork or protect them with a heater guard.

Bogwood

Bogwood is ideal for aquarium decoration and suited to nearly every aquascape. Bogwood, as its name suggests, is wood that has been dug up from various waterlogged sites. Over time, the wood has become twisted and shaped and completely reformed. A piece of bogwood not only provides excellent retreats and hiding places for fish, but can also become a striking object in the aquarium. Use it as a centrepiece or just have the odd branch coming from nowhere in the background or on the substrate.

There are various types of wood available and it is worth keeping an eye on what is in stock, as batches of bogwood change quite often. Choose carefully and try to imagine where the wood will fit into your design. Commercially prepared woods are often smoothed and cleaned and have a more solid feel. They are both equally good and provide a useful choice. Try not to mix different types of bogwood in one aquarium as this very rarely looks effective.

As bogwood is sold dry, you will occasionally come across a piece that will not sink. In this case, soak it in a bucket of water for several days. If it still does not sink, you may need to anchor it with sealant or replace it. Most bogwood will stain the water a slight brown-yellow colour due to the release of tannic acids. Again, soaking it for a few days before placing it in the aquarium can help to reduce this effect.

The tannic acids released into the water can reduce the pH level, making it more acidic. This is beneficial to most fish and plants, which prefer slightly acidic

Synthetic tank decorations

This fake bark is a good shape for hiding internal filters and heaters.

This piece looks natural and will not alter the colour of the water.

This realistic rock is inert and safe to use in any aquarium.

Fake wood is available in attractive and manageable sizes.

conditions. In the wild, many bodies of water would have this brown-yellow staining from tannic acids. In the aquarium, the colour staining of the water by bogwood can actually add to the overall effect. However, if the coloration is not wanted, it is easy to remove, either by regular water changes or by using carbon in the aquarium filter for short periods.

Do not use normal wood in an aquarium, as it will rot and release toxins, as well as considerably reducing oxygen levels. Bogwood is the remaining core after the rest of the wood has rotted away, so it is safe and will not decay. Normal

wood can only be used if it is first treated with a polyurethane varnish.

Naturally fake

Because of the problems associated with rocks that may affect the water chemistry, bogwood that stains the water yellow and the difficulty of finding attractive pieces, a number of synthetic decors are now available. Some of these synthetic woods and rocks can look very convincing and, once established in the aquarium, with algae growing over the surface, they become almost indistinguishable from the real thing. Some pieces are designed to conceal filter inlet pipes or heater/thermostats, by covering them with a realistic-looking tree root. Take care when hiding heater/thermostats; remember that you need a good flow around the heater to maintain a steady temperature throughout the aquarium.

Another form of synthetic decor is spray-on rock. This novel idea allows you to spray on a rocky background or create caves out of foam, which will then set hard. It allows you to create some very interesting objects, although the final result is never as realistic as you may have hoped for.

Fake decor is available in many forms, but it is quite expensive and many pieces are far from perfect. However, you can be sure that it is safe to use in the aquarium. Finally, remember that some algae-eating fish need real wood as part of their diet and may not survive without it.

Natural decor

Other objects can be used in the aquarium to good effect as natural decor. For example, if you were to create a Malaysian swamp, you may well use bamboo canes. Bamboo is very cheap, available from garden centres and if used correctly brings life to an underwater scene. Other useful materials include snail shells, plastic plants, clay pots (preferably broken), thin bush branches (no leaves), twigs and even cork bark.

Securing the decor

If you are creating a very rocky scene, with rocks stacked quite high, consider using a silicone sealant to fix them in place. Silicone sealant is incredibly strong and works with virtually any material. Make sure that the objects you are sticking together are dry and free from dust.

Gluing rocks with silicone

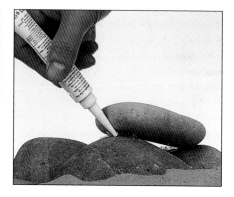

1 When you have decided where the rocks are to go, silicone them into place. Squeeze large beads of silicone onto any hard, clean surface.

2 Fill any gaps between the rocks with more silicone. Do not worry if the silicone is visible, it can be trimmed away quite easily when it is dry.

'dry run' first so that you know exactly which pieces go where. Removing wet silicone is virtually impossible and very messy.

Above: This rockface was constructed some days before the tank was filled with water. All the rocks were siliconed to each other and to the rear glass of the tank.

Use as much sealant as necessary and leave the objects to dry for three or four days in a well-ventilated area.

Silicone sealant can also be used to help secure items of decor that usually float in the aquarium. Fix bark or dried-out bogwood to rocks, slate or a sheet of glass. Place the sheets of glass or slate beneath the substrate so that only the emerging bark or wood is visible.

If you are feeling ambitious, you can even create waterfalls and caves using silicone sealants. Carry out a

Creating a background

Gazing into an aquarium is like seeing into another world and can easily become quite entrancing. But if you look a little deeper and spot net curtains or flowery wallpaper, the effect is ruined. That is why a good background is so important. A background isolates and 'holds' the aquatic world within the aquarium.

Backgrounds are available in many forms. The most common one is the sheet plastic available in black or blue or in a number of designs, ranging from simple planted aquascapes to Roman ruins and even 3D-effect rockwork. For the most natural effect, use a black backing combined with good lighting. Together, they will show up the decor and the fish within the aquarium.

Backgrounds are also available to fit inside the aquarium. Many are made to standard sizes, designed to fit most aquariums. They are often a textured moulded plastic, mimicking a rockface. These backgrounds must be fixed inside the aquarium when it is dry and empty, as they are tricky to add later on. When you install the background, make sure that it joins correctly; there is nothing worse than a visible line straight down the middle of two sheets.

Finally, you can create your own background from rocks, bogwood, bark or any safe material you like. It is quite hard to cover the entire back of the aquarium without taking up too much room, so you may need to use a black plastic backing as well. Remember that not all the background will be seen, especially if you plan to incorporate heavy planting in your design.

It is not a good idea to paint the outside glass of the tank. This is a rather drastic measure and hard to reverse. Over time, the paint on the glass will begin to crack and peel, leaving clear spots at the back of the aquarium. By this time, the aquarium is likely to be in a place where it will not be easy to repaint.

Laying the foundations

The key principle of aquascaping is to make the best possible use of all the resources you have. Everything that goes into the aquarium will

Above: Washing gravel is a laborious but essential task. Gravel is full of dust and debris that will cloud the water, so wash it thoroughly before placing it in the tank.

contribute to its overall look. The substrate's primary function is to support rocks and other decor and provide a home for plants to root in, but it can also become a very important piece of decor itself.

First and foremost, you must wash the substrate thoroughly to remove dust and debris. This is quite possibly one of the most tedious jobs you will ever have to do, but it must be done properly. Some substrates, such as silver sand, are virtually impossible to wash, so they can go directly into the aquarium. Other substrates should be rinsed in small buckets under a tap in handfuls at a time until the water runs clear. Once this is done, place the substrate into the aquarium so that it is flat and even across the base.

This becomes the starting point for moulding and shaping the substrate into an undulating and exciting landscape. Try to pile some substrate at the rear of the aquarium and create small hills and raised areas. Use rocks to stagger the substrate, creating many different layers. Raised areas can be used to good effect for planting, and piling up substrate against rocks reproduces the effect seen in many river beds, where the rocks have 'caught' sediment in the oncoming flow. Using rocks to keep the substrate in place will help to stop fish from levelling the ground, which they will do over time. Roots and bogwood can also be used in the same way. If you plan to use plants in your design, allow at least 5-7.5cm (2-3in) of substrate in any planting areas.

Rockwork

Once the substrate is firmly in place, the next step is to add the larger objects that will become key features of the finished design. When adding rocks, always start with the largest one and place it in a dominant position in the tank. Do not place key items directly in the centre, as this looks highly unnatural. Instead, position them to one side as if they were put there by accident. If you have two or even three large rocks, make sure they all vary slightly in size and do not space them equally.

If you are using a number of rocks, you may wish to grade them by placing smaller rocks by the side of larger ones. This helps to soften the effect of the large rocks without removing any of their dominant status, and it also stops large rocks from looking as if they have appeared from nowhere.

Different types of rocks can be used in the same display, but rocks of the same type will look more natural. It may be worth breaking up some rocks into small pieces to scatter near the larger rocks or mix with the main substrate. Again, this helps to incorporate the large rocks into the whole display. If you are using rocks to create a stacked background or the scene is dominated by piled rock, it is important to place these rocks as they would be in nature. Think about the process that produces these rockscapes in the wild. As the rocks fall, they 'fit' into gaps and spaces left by other rocks. They would not be balanced, but firmly wedged in place and this is what you should try to achieve in the aquarium: a firm

Right: Rocks with unusual lines or patterns look attractive in the aquarium. The rocks shown here are all various types and sizes of slate. Sticking to one type of rock usually creates a better display than mixing different ones.

Above: This piece of bogwood, combined with the sand substrate, rocks and plants, creates a good focal point in the tank display. The natural curve also provides an ideal hiding place for fish.

system of rocks that fit together and become very hard to remove.

Rocks are also very important to the fish, because small gaps in the rockwork provide safe retreats and secure hiding places. Remember that the more hiding places you give your fish, the more you will see them out and about. This is because once they are familiar with their environment, they will know exactly where to hide from a predator or other emergency. Even if the caves cannot be seen in the final display, make them an essential part of the aquarium.

Bogwood and roots

Wood has an equally important role in the aquarium, providing hiding places and territories for the fish, as well as being key objects in the decor. In many aquariums it is better to have long, thin pieces, rather than thick, bulky ones. You can use more pieces and they take up less space. Again, think about where the wood would be in nature. Place curved wood in the substrate with both ends buried, creating the illusion that there is more to it and maybe it is a root from a nearby tree. If you are using plants quite heavily, wood can look very effective just visible above a dense group of plants.

Bogwood can also be used as a rooting medium for plants such as *Anubias* sp., Java fern *(Microsorium*

Above: Java fern (Microsorium pteropus) is an excellent aquarium plant that prefers to grow on rocks and wood than in the aquarium substrate.

pteropus) and Java moss *(Vesicularia dubyana)*, which will root and spread over the wood.

To create the effect of overhanging roots, fix wood to the top of the aquarium, either suspended from a removable support or fixed with sealant to the side of the aquarium. Allow one or two roots from the surface to reach the substrate, with others at varying heights above. Alternatively, stretching a couple of long pieces across most of the aquarium's length can look most

impressive. Incorporating wood like this really creates the feeling that a part of nature has been sliced away and placed inside the aquarium.

Twigs can also be used to create the impression of branches from an overhanging tree, but make sure that branches are clean and free of leaves. If you are using real wood and twigs rather than bogwood, try not to use wood more than 1cm (0.4in) in diameter and, if possible, use dead wood. Larger diameter branches are more likely to release dangerous resins and toxins into the water. Twigs and branches will eventually rot and must be replaced regularly unless treated with a non-toxic polyurethane varnish.

Green fingers

Now that the substrate, rocks and wood are in place it is time to plant the aquarium. Choosing the correct plants for your display is very important. They must be the right size and shape and should contrast with one other. Take into account that the plants will grow when planning where to position them.

If you think about plants in nature, you are more likely to see a few dominant species together, rather than many different varieties in one area. But having just one species in the aquarium can be rather boring, so the solution is a compromise: a limited number of species planted in groups throughout the aquarium is usually the best option.

The rocks and wood already in the aquarium will provide either a backdrop for smaller plants or a foreground for the larger varieties. Place large bushy plants at the rear of the aquarium and hide the lower half of the plant. Small foreground plants can be used to good effect if they are spread over an open area and around small stones or wood. Small-leaved varieties of *Anubias nana* are perfect for rooting on small pieces of wood in the foreground. Do the same with Java moss, which works well in fast-flowing river displays. Place Java fern at the top of bogwood and grow it above other plants. If you allow Java fern to spread, it will cover whole rock faces and create a dense mat of vegetation.

Try not to overdo the planting and, with the exception of very small varieties, place the plants as far back as possible in the aquarium. It is important to distinguish between 'specimen' plants and plants that should be grouped. Generally speaking, specimen plants have large, rounded leaves and stand out from other plants. Place these centrally and give them their own space. Plants with fine, bushy or small,

Left: This Anubias *sp. is a small plant with attractive foliage. Once fastened or wedged into wood or rock, it will slowly spread across any available surface.*

rounded leaves usually look best in groups towards the rear of the tank.

To keep plants in top condition, regularly add a good-quality fertilizer, preferably one that contains iron, and reduce oxygen levels by lowering the outlet to your filter and minimizing surface movement.

Planting in adverse conditions
Sometimes it is hard to use real plants in aquariums because the conditions are too unfavourable. Hard water, undergravel filtration, high oxygen levels and plant-eating fish can all ruin displays. There are a few solutions to these problems.

Some plants are much hardier than others, so do a bit of research and choose robust varieties. *Egeria* sp., *Elodea* sp., *Hygrophila corymbosa*, *Vallisneria spiralis* (straight vallis), *Microsorium pteropus* (Java fern) and many *Cryptocoryne* species adapt readily to hard water and high oxygen levels. A few, such as *Vallisneria* sp.

and *Microsorium* sp. can also be kept in brackish conditions, although their success depends on a number of variables. In displays with plant-eating or destructive fish, there is only one plant with any chance of survival – Java fern. It produces a substance in its leaves that is distasteful to many fish, so most fish learn to avoid it, even plant-eaters.

If you are using undergravel filtration in your display, then plants may do better inside pots under the substrate. The best method is to place a tray or slate under the substrate that will stop the flow of water in that area. Of course, you cannot do this too much, as it will inhibit the usefulness of the filter.

Finally, if all else fails, you can always revert to plastic alternatives. Choose plastic plants carefully, as

Below: Details can make a display. Here, a small piece of bogwood appears to be part of a tree root and blends naturally with the sand and pebbles around it.

some look far from real. Most aquatic centres will have a number of plastic plants in sales tanks to make the fish feel more comfortable. Have a look at these to get an idea of how the plants will look in your tank.

Planting above water

One very pleasing effect is to allow plants to grow out of the water. This can be achieved in an aquarium without a hood and with suspended lighting. It is also possible to use terrestrial plants above the tank and incorporate them into the display.

Some terrestrial bog plants will live quite happily with their roots submerged in water. The roots will be clearly visible in the aquarium and add to the display, as well as offering hiding places for fish. Many aquatic plants will also grow to the surface and beyond; they may even flower out of the water if given the chance. Aquariums that are only half-filled or have visible land areas can benefit from terrestrial plants. Some mosses and alpines will grow in small cracks of exposed rockwork, creeping over bare rock and even into the water.

Blending everything together

With all the major components in place, it is time to add the finishing touches. At this stage, the display should be pretty impressive; the aim now is to make it spectacular. So far, by using natural materials and plants, we have been faithful to the idea of a natural aquarium. But everything has been planned and carefully placed. This does not happen in nature, so we need to add a bit of randomness, some mess and debris and bits of decor that appear to serve no purpose.

Start by blending and grading the substrate. Depending on your chosen substrate, try to use some larger or smaller pieces and sprinkle them unevenly across the aquarium floor. Leave some areas untouched and cover others with larger stones. If you are using pea gravel, add some larger grades and small pebbles. Pile up the larger grades around the pebbles. If your substrate is quite light, add a few sprinklings of a darker substrate and vice-versa.

If your aquarium has quite a rocky theme, break up some rocks of the type you are using and scatter these pieces around the base of the large pieces. Do the same with bogwood; find some smaller pieces (under 15cm/6in) and scatter these around the substrate. Part-bury some and leave others exposed. Many retailers throw away these small broken pieces, so you should be able to get them for next to nothing.

Finally, take a look at the plants in the aquarium. Are they all the same height? Do they look as if they have been deliberately placed? Trim groups of tall plants so that they are all differing lengths, with smaller plants on the outside of the group and tall ones at the back. Foreground plants look good in groups, but to achieve a natural look, stagger them slightly. Most foreground plants consist of a clump of very small plants, so separate a few individuals and place them near the main group as if they had spread outwards.

A MOUNTAIN STREAM

Where the mighty river systems begin, small trickles of water combine to form streams. The soil is thin and the streams easily carve channels down to the bedrock. The water here is clean, crisp and undiluted by organic matter.

In times of rain, the larger permanent mountain streams become raging rivers, falling down the steep landscape. When the rains finish and summer arrives the water disappears, leaving a stream that looks quite lost in the centre of a dried riverbed. At this time, larger fish are found further downstream or in pools and lakes connected to the streams.

Naturally pure

The crystal clear water of a mountain stream tumbles chaotically over bare rock in a form that can only be described as nature at its purest.

Adapt and survive
The fish in these mountain streams and rivers have to be adapted to both slow-moving water and raging,

powerful flows, depending on the time of year. Most fish are small, with streamlined bodies, such as the White Cloud Mountain minnow *(Tanichthys albonubes)*, named after the White Cloud Mountain in southern China where it is found. Temperatures underwater are often fluctuating, with rainfall at lower temperatures than the normal river waters. Many fish from tropical mountain streams are temperate and may not need heating in an indoor aquarium. Fish such as the Chinese hillstream loach *(Pseudogastromyzon cheni)* are well adapted to flowing water. Their dynamic body shape allows them to cling to rocks and feed off the algae that grows plentifully in these areas.

A tough life for plants

Predators are not often larger fish, but more likely to be birds and mountain animals that readily fish for a meal. Luckily there are usually plenty of hiding places amongst rocks and roots. However, plant cover is not so readily available, as conditions in the mountains are unfavourable for growth. The water is often hard and alkaline due to the low levels of organic matter and from minerals picked up as it flows over bedrock. With the streams fluctuating in size annually, plants do not have time to establish themselves and the fast-flowing water and high oxygen levels just make life harder for any aquatic foliage.

Algae and mosses are the dominant foliage in these areas. They will cover most rocks and thrive in small pools and marshes alongside the main stream. This life provides food for most fish, not just through the plant matter but through the tiny animals and infusoria that live amongst the vegetation. Other food comes in the form of small creatures such as insect larvae, amphipods and other filter feeders. The most basic of food chains is found in these mountain stream habitats.

The mountain aquarium

In the aquarium, the best way to convey the water movement and rocky surroundings is to be able to see the water coming into the tank. We can achieve this by only filling two-thirds of the aquarium and constructing a waterfall at one end.

Right: The striped barb (Barbus eugrammus) *is a classic stream fish. Notice how the body is a streamlined torpedo shape to minimize drag in fast-moving waters. Despite its confident and active behaviour, this is a timid fish in the aquarium.*

A sufficiently powerful pump will produce a strong flow of water and really capture the spirit of the mountain stream.

The substrate

In a normal mountain stream, the substrate would be a mixture of bare rock and gravel. In this aquarium, we have used silver sand for two reasons. Firstly, the rockwork is quite heavy and needs a firm base; silver sand is ideal for this. Secondly, the smaller flat stones and the carefully placed gravel are seen to best effect on a silver sand base. However, you could just as easily use a medium-grade gravel as the main substrate, making sure that the rocks are well supported. We have sprinkled a medium-grade pea gravel across the aquarium floor. Try to group this in some areas, as if the water flow has separated it from the finer sand. Do not use too many types of substrate; try to stick to a basic look.

Use large pieces of slate with a solid, angular appearance to create a waterfall feature.

Rockwork

In this display, we have used slate, which is a dark and shapely rock that enhances the powerful feel of the waterfall. The pieces are large and 'chunky' in appearance, which means they are also very heavy, so take care when placing them. As you build the rockwork above the water, try to create dips and cracks that can be sealed and filled with a small amount of earth for the terrestrial plants. The smaller rocks are also slate, but in a slightly different form. These pieces are rounded and smoother, but they still

Smaller, rounded pieces of slate placed across the aquarium floor look as if they have been worn smooth by the flow of water.

retain the fracturing scars that identify them as slate. The effect is of broken pieces of larger rock that have found their way to the stream bed and been smoothed by the constant erosion of flowing water. Place these in a random pattern, but cover as much of the substrate as possible. Some pieces can be half buried, as if they have just been exposed by the moving sediment.

These alpine plants are found in the mountain stream environment and will thrive in the aquarium. This is Sedum rupestre.

Arenaria caespitosa 'Aurea'

Bogwood

A few pieces of bogwood soften the overall look, but they are not vital and should not be used as key items in the display, rather as finishing touches. Sometimes, wood is available with Java moss attached, which adds a hint of plant life. The moss will move in the flow and convey the power of the water.

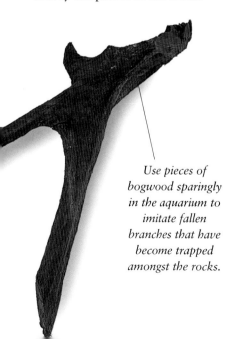

Use pieces of bogwood sparingly in the aquarium to imitate fallen branches that have become trapped amongst the rocks.

Plant life

Remember, life is hard for the plants in this rocky environment. Apart from Java moss, we have used no other aquatic plants. Instead, we have planted above the water. Alpines are ideal for this purpose and the two varieties included here – *Sedum rupestre (reflexum)* and *Arenaria caespitosa* 'Aurea' – will thrive in these conditions. They do not require a mass of soil to root in and will happily grow out of small cracks between rocks. In time, they spread across the rockwork right up to the edge of the water. Other terrestrial plants can be potted above the aquarium, leaving branches and leaves to droop down into the tank.

The waterfall

This is the key feature of the display and should be created with care. In this 90cm (36in) aquarium we have used a powerhead capable of pumping about 1600 litres of water per hour. Considering that in this setup the aquarium only holds about 80 litres of water, this is a turnover of 20 times per hour, which is quite a high flow rate.

The waterfall is made up of two parts. The first is a fixed housing for the pump, secured in position with silicone sealant inside the aquarium. This is the waterfall up to the point where the water arrives. On top of this you can place the second half of the waterfall, a 'lid', where the water will overflow into the aquarium. This part should also be siliconed together, but not into the tank, as you will need to remove it to reach the pump. Make sure that the 'lid' directs the flow precisely, otherwise a shaft of water will shoot across the whole tank. If the flow is incorrectly

The mountain stream aquarium

Position houseplants above or behind the aquarium. The overhanging leaves will imitate terrestrial vegetation and the plant will enjoy water sprayed from the waterfall.

This piece of bogwood 'plays the part' of a sunken tree root.

These large rocks are heavy and sharp and could be dangerous if not siliconed firmly in place.

Java moss grows on almost any surface and as it sways it will help to project the image of a fast-moving stream.

redirected, it may end up spraying all over the front glass of the tank, making it impossible to clean. Finally, remember to place a small sponge on the pump inlet, just in case any fish get inside the waterfall.

The fish

Compared to the larger river habitats, relatively few varieties of fish are found in the mountain stream environment, but this does not mean that there are few fish to choose from. As this display need not be area specific, we can quite happily mix fish from different regions.

Most mountain streams will vary in temperature throughout the year and are generally cooler than other tropical waters. Many of the fish

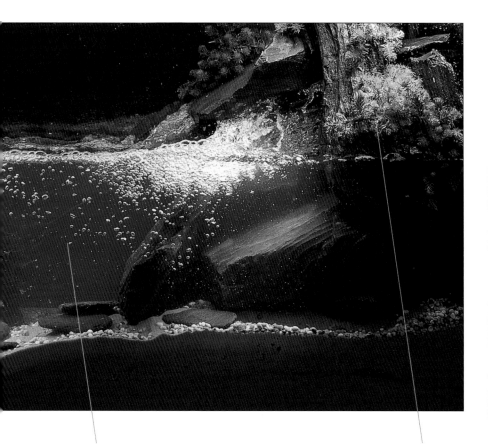

The open water area is perfect for the fish to swim against the flow, while the rockwork provides quiet retreats.

These alpines need little planting substrate and will thrive here, creeping over the rocks onto the water surface.

suited to this setup may appreciate slightly lower temperatures than normal. Nearly all mountain stream fish are relatively peaceful and constantly active. The combination of highly active fish and fast water movement makes this an exhilarating display to look into.

Feisty barbs

Many barbs are ideally suited to a fast-flowing environment such as this. Barbs are very social fish, so keep them in groups. They appear to be constantly fighting amongst themselves, but do not worry; real harm very rarely occurs. Despite their active nature and apparent confidence, many barbs are, in fact, quite timid and easily frightened. They will need dark hiding places to retreat to. Popular barbs suited to this set-up include the rosy barb *(Barbus conchonius)*, striped barb *(Barbus eugrammus)* and the two-spot barb *(Barbus ticto)*

Below: The small size and streamlined shape of the minnow (Phoxinus phoxinus) *enables it to dart against the flow, catching any food that passes by.*

Danios

One of the most popular and widely available aquarium fish is the zebra danio *(Brachydanio rerio)*. This small fish will zoom around the aquarium, always on the move. Zebra danios are amazingly fast swimmers that love the strong flow in the mountain stream aquarium. Danios will also spawn quite readily in the right conditions, although the young rarely survive in a fully stocked aquarium.

Streamlined by nature

A number of catfish are adapted to live in fast-flowing environments. Most of them are algae eaters and have strong mouths designed for attaching to rocks to graze. The Otocinclus group of small catfish are excellent algae-eaters and a welcome addition to any aquarium. In nature they are found in flowing waters, but are incredibly versatile and unfussy about tank conditions.

Some of the adaptations made by fish to survive fast-flowing waters can result in unusual and interesting body shapes. The giant whiptail catfish *(Sturisoma aureum)* has developed massive fins in order to

hold position and generate the power to move against the flow in this environment. The whiptail catfish are very peaceful, but are also loners by nature and may not appreciate a heavily stocked aquarium.

Some loaches are also ideally suited to this environment. One of the best, the Chinese hillstream loach *(Pseudogastromyzon cheni)*, is a small fish with a flat rounded body that looks almost as if it has been stood on. It is at home clinging to rocks while the water flows over its compressed body. The hillstream loach is also well camouflaged and often hard to spot.

Mountain minnows

An old favourite and the original mountain stream fish has to be the

Above: The dwarf otocinclus (Otocinclus affinis) *is a small peaceful fish that will happily move around the tank grazing algae from rocks. Ideally, keep a shoal of these fish in the aquarium.*

minnow *(Phoxinus phoxinus)*. This small, native European fish is only rarely available, but ideal for this display. It is a peaceful shoaling fish and should be kept in groups. Another minnow (although only by common name) is the White Cloud Mountain minnow *(Tanichthys albonubes)*. This tiny, colourful fish is hardy and undemanding and one of the easiest to keep. Attractive long-finned varieties are also available, but being tank-bred, they may not be the ideal choice for a truly natural aquarium.

A Central American Stream

The clear lowland streams of Central America are home to many livebearers that spend their time hunting small insects and mosquito larvae. In some areas there is lush but patchy vegetation, an ideal backdrop to recreate in the aquarium.

Conditions in the lowland streams are not always ideal for aquatic plants and vegetation is often sparse. However, in calmer areas of the stream, dense groups of plants can be found along the banks and in shallow areas. Each stream throughout this relatively small area is unique. The landscape has created a wide array of natural water bodies in the form of numerous swamps, streams, lagoons and rivers. Depending on the location, streams can be clear and fast-flowing over rocks and pebbles or idle creeks gently flowing over a substrate of sand, mud and leaf debris.

Tropical paradise

In many areas, dense vegetation provides food in the form of fruit and seeds and aquatic animals that feed on fallen and rotting vegetation.

Not quite the Amazon

Whereas the Amazonian streams and backwaters are acidic and soft – an ideal environment for vegetation – the Central American streams are the exact opposite: alkaline and hard.

These conditions are caused by the soil and rock, which are full of calcareous material. Many areas lie on a base of limestone rock, which raises hardness up to as much as 50°dGH and the pH level very rarely drops below 7.

Natural exterminators

The diet of many of the fish that inhabit the Central American streams is based mainly on insects and mosquito larvae. In fact, some fish, such as the mosquitofish *(Gambusia affinis)* and the guppy *(Poecilia reticulata),* have been deliberately introduced into other areas to control mosquito populations. Other foods available in these streams include algae and many small aquatic invertebrates. Catfish such as *Pimelodus pictus* can be found darting along the stream bed searching for small animals amongst the substrate. In areas with cover provided either by tree roots, overhanging banks or vegetation,

Above: Catfish, such as this Pimelodus pictus *can be found at the stream bed, rushing around in a constant search for food in the gravelly substrate.*

smaller fish can be found hunting insects and bugs. Given the small size and shallow nature of the streams, there are relatively few aquatic predators. Most natural predators are land-based birds and mammals that readily fish the streams in search of a meal.

The substrate

The Mexican streams are not far from their sources and consequently have not had time to build up sediment, leaving a gravel substrate mixed with a few larger rocks and pebbles. If you plan to plant heavily, use a fine grade of gravel or mix grades so that the largest is at the top. You may wish to use a little coral gravel or other calcareous substrate to buffer the water a little, keeping it slightly hard and alkaline.

Rockwork

There is very little rockwork in this aquarium apart from a cobble here and there, but larger rounded rocks would complement the display well. Grade the larger cobbles or small rocks and scatter small pebbles randomly across the substrate. Try to use light and dark pebbles so that some stand out more than others against the similarly coloured gravel. As with the substrate, you can add limestone or other calcareous rocks to maintain hard, alkaline water conditions.

Wood

The wood here represents roots from the stream bank. In this aquarium, a few long pieces are stretched across the background of the aquarium and also hide the heater/thermostat.

Plants

There are only five species of plant in this aquarium. In the wild, you would be unlikely to find many species in a small area in this

A substrate of medium-grade pea gravel is ideal for this setup.

type of habitat. The plants here are grouped, separated and bunched together. When choosing plants for this display, bear in mind that the ideal water quality for the fish in this habitat is not ideal for most plants. Select hardy plant varieties that will accept slightly hard and alkaline water. Plants such as *Cabomba caroliniana* (green cabomba) are ideal for the background. In deep aquariums, dense groups planted towards the back of the aquarium are very effective. Cabomba is a hardy plant and once established, you can take cuttings from it to replant in the substrate. *Vallisneria spiralis* (straight vallis) makes an excellent contrast to cabomba.

These large pebbles match the substrate in shape and colour.

Its tall, slender leaves are ideal for the livebearers that graze among them, removing algae. *Vallisneria spiralis* is one of the most widespread aquatic plants because it is so adaptable and quickly reproduces.

Maintaining water quality

If you do not use any rocks or substrates to maintain slightly hard and alkaline conditions, then carry out regular small water changes and regular gravel cleaning. This will reduce the build-up of organic matter, which may lower the pH level and water hardness.

Given reasonably bright lighting levels, Cabomba *sp. will grow rapidly and provide an elegant display of feathery fronds.*

This attractive Hygrophila *sp. looks best when planted in groups.*

The fish

The Central American streams are home mainly to small cichlids, livebearers and some characins. Most of these fish are peaceful and create a good community aquarium. Many of the livebearers will benefit from the addition of a little salt to the tank, but this of course depends on the other inhabitants and plants in the aquarium.

Livebearers

Due to their hardy nature, the common livebearers are known to virtually all fishkeepers. These fish, along with some tetras, are widely recommended as ideal 'first fish' for beginners. Their peaceful behaviour, bright colours and highly reproductive nature make them interesting and worthwhile fish for any community aquarium. The best

51

known livebearer is the guppy *(Poecilia reticulata)*. It is available in many different tank-bred varieties, with greatly enhanced finnage and coloration. It is also sporadically available in its natural wild form.

Another favourite livebearer is the platy *(Xiphophorus maculatus)*. It is found mainly in the fresh and brackish waters of Mexico. In the same habitat you will also find the molly *(Poecilia sphenops)*. When kept in purely fresh water, this slightly larger livebearer can be prone to health problems, but in the correct hard, alkaline conditions it should remain healthy and active. Various species of molly are available, including the stunning sailfin molly *(Poecilia velifera)*, which has a huge

The Central American stream aquarium

This piece of bogwood is mostly hidden behind a wall of plants, made up of straight vallis (Vallisneria spiralis) *and* Hygrophila sp. Vallisneria spiralis *will quickly reach the surface.*

The Java moss (Vesicularia dubyana) *on this wood is an interesting addition to the aquarium.*

Blend larger cobbles with small pebbles to create a group of rocks.

dorsal fin that is used for displays between rival males and as a courtship display.

The swordtail *(Xiphophorus helleri)* is similar in shape to the mollies and platies. It gets its name from the male fish's swordlike extension to the caudal (tail) fin. If environmental factors require it, it is possible for a female swordtail to change sex and this happens quite often. It can occur if the population is mainly female or if the female ages and her eggs are not as fertile.

Finally, an interesting and different livebearer is the pike livebearer, or piketop minnow, *(Belonesox belizanus).* This predator feeds primarily on small fish, hiding behind roots and plants waiting to

Randomly placed pebbles make the substrate look more natural.

These foreground plants are small Echinodorus *sp.*

Grouping plants with contrasting leaf shapes can create a striking effect.

strike. As it will only grow to about 10cm (4in), it can be kept together with fish of a similar size or larger.

Breeding livebearers

Bear in mind that most livebearers are prolific breeders and although it is always nice to have fish breed in the aquarium, it may be better to try and prevent it. After mating, the females may produce a number of broods and, providing there is a suitable male and female, they will continue to produce young. In a community tank, the young are often eaten before they have a chance to grow, but if they do survive, they may overrun the tank. To stop fish breeding, keeping one sex is the best option. If you plan to breed or mix sexes, bear in mind that many male livebearers seem to have only two aims in life: feeding and breeding. Constant attention will stress some females; to reduce this risk, keep at least twice as many females as males.

Above: The mosquitofish (Gambusia affinis) *is an unusual, active fish. This male will grow no more than 2.5cm (1in), but females grow to over 7.5cm (3in).*

Catfish

An ideal fish to inhabit the lower reaches of the aquarium would be the pictus catfish *(Pimelodus pictus)*. This peaceful and active fish will grow no bigger than 10cm (4in). It is not nocturnal, but constantly active during the day, sweeping the substrate in search of food.

Left: The guppy (Poecilia reticulata) *is possibly the best-known tropical freshwater fish, but most guppies available to fishkeepers are tank-bred varieties with enhanced colour and finnage. This is the wild coloration, which can vary from one location to another.*

Above: *The piketop minnow (Belonesox belizanus) has a powerful jaw that is used for catching passing prey. In the aquarium, this fish will spend its time hiding amongst plants waiting for a meal.*

Left: *The swordtail (Xiphophorus helleri) is a hardy livebearer that will grow up to 12cm (4.7in) in an aquarium. Only the male fish possesses the swordlike extension to the caudal fin.*

A CENTRAL AMERICAN RIVER

As the streams of Central America converge into larger rivers, a new habitat is created. These rivers are home to the 'guapotes', or giant predators. Large cichlids, aggressive and territorial by nature, live and breed in these waters.

Under rocky terrain

The waters that swirl around these rocks create an active underwater environment in which the Central American cichlids thrive.

The Central American, or Meso-American, landbridge is a rocky, volcanic landscape. The rivers here are relatively short from source to mouth and the steep, rocky terrain means they are often fast-flowing. In the rainy season, the large rivers become raging torrents and any underlying soil is quickly removed, leaving a bed of rocks and large gravel. The water in these rivers is often hard and alkaline. Minerals are picked up from the rocks and the abundant calcareous limestone raises hardness and pH levels. Since

organic debris is quickly washed away, there is a lack of acidification (softening) of the water.

Algae to go
In sunlit areas, this rocky underwater landscape is perfect for the development of algae, the main source of food for many of the fish.

Left: In common with many cichlids from this area, the firemouth cichlid (Cichlasoma meeki), exhibits strong parental instincts and will vigorously defend and protect its young. In the aquarium they will confidently attack any intruder - on either side of the glass!

Some of the cichlids here, as with many Lake Malawi cichlids, have adapted mouths to rasp algae from the surface of the rocks. Other food sources for fish are available in the form of crustaceans, aquatic animals, insects and insect larvae and, in calmer areas, plant debris.

The boundaries of nature

Many of the cichlids in these rivers are highly territorial, mainly during the breeding season when aggression is used to attract mates and protect young fry. Distinguishable rocks, roots and any other noticeable objects are used as boundaries.

Parental care

After the rains have come and as the water temperature begins to creep up, it is time to start breeding. At this time of year the water is clear and high, food sources are abundant and suitable breeding sites are readily available in the shallows. Most cichlids here breed in a similar fashion. The male first selects a mate from the surrounding population and finds a suitable substrate for egg-laying. The fish pair up and begin to bond, forming a territory. The eggs are usually laid on a flat rock or other surface to which they will adhere, and then fertilized by the male. The cichlids here are good parents and will defend the eggs and brood in a breeding site of up to 3m (10ft) across. Initially, the female is usually in charge of the eggs and fry and will keep a close eye on them, rarely straying more than 1m (39in) away. The male will defend the larger territory, preventing predators from coming anywhere near the young. When the fry are hatched they stay close to their parents. The young are often moved up and down the warmer banks of the river, where abundant sources of zooplankton and phytoplankton provide excellent food for the young fish.

Lagoons

In the Central American region there are also many lagoons and craters where cichlids and other fish can be found. Many of these pools vary dramatically in size throughout the year and offer good habitats for breeding and feeding.

Place smaller pebbles like these across the substrate.

Rockwork

Most types of rock can be used in this aquarium. The form of slate used here is ideal for creating large caves, and the flat sides make excellent breeding and egglaying sites for cichlids. Take extreme care with these large, heavy rocks. Some of the larger cichlids can be quite destructive at times and are quite capable of moving large rocks, thus increasing the danger of falling rockwork and cracked aquariums. Any large rocks not firmly bedded and immovable in the substrate should be siliconed securely into place. As before, blend in the

The substrate

Pea gravel is the best medium for this aquarium. It should be fairly thick to support the weight of the larger rocks. Avoid sharp substrates to protect the fishes' mouths. Many Central American cichlids have a tendency to dig, which is natural breeding behaviour but can be annoying and dangerous in an aquarium, especially if a fish decides to dig underneath a large rock. To solve this problem, use a gravel tidy, a simple plastic mesh placed in the substrate below which the fish cannot dig. Place a layer of fine or medium grade pea gravel on the base of the aquarium as normal and cover it with the gravel tidy. Arrange the rocks on the gravel tidy and cover any open space with a final layer of medium or large-grade pea gravel.

These large pieces of slate are heavy. Take great care when you place them in the aquarium.

This plastic guard will protect the heater from rocks and fish.

rocks by scattering smaller, rounded pieces across the substrate. A good strategy is to smash (carefully) one of the larger rocks into small pieces and place these randomly around the base of the larger rocks.

Wood and plants

You can if you wish add large pieces of bogwood to this aquarium, but here we have kept to a basic, rocky formula. There is a piece of wood in this tank, but it is well hidden and only serves the purpose of a rooting medium for the Java fern. This fern is a feathered, short variety (*Microsorium pteropus* 'Windelov'), which creates a bushier-looking plant than the natural strain. The large cichlids in this type of setup will happily destroy most plants, so heavy planting is not a good idea. As well as Java fern, you can use robust plants such as the Amazon sword (*Echinodorus* sp.) or *Anubias* species.

Special notes

The cichlids suited to this aquarium are very messy eaters that create a lot of waste. Be sure to install adequate filtration to maintain constantly good water quality in the tank, and clean the substrate regularly with an aquarium gravel cleaner.

When positioning the decor, remember that, as in nature, the fish will use objects within the tank as boundaries and territory markers. Make sure you create enough caves and distinctive areas for all the inhabitants to have their own 'area'. If there are problems with aggression, then moving the decor and, therefore, the territories, often

This variety of Java fern (Microsorium pteropus 'Windelov') has very attractive 'feathered' leaves.

helps. As well as moving rocks, big cichlids are capable of breaking any equipment in the aquarium. The item most likely to be broken is the glass heater/thermostat, so in this aquarium it is protected from the attentions of the fish by a guard. In this situation, it is worth paying a little extra and using a reinforced glass heater/thermostat, just in case.

The fish

Central American cichlids make perfect display fish. Their large size and stunning colours mean that they are always the focus of attention in the aquarium. They also seem to have strong personalities and individual behavioural traits, which explains why many fishkeepers give their own specimens 'pet' names.

The Central American river aquarium

Large upright rocks like this can be siliconed to the aquarium glass.

Java fern will produce 'baby plants' from its leaves. You can remove these and wedge them into cracks in the rockwork, where they will root and spread.

This substrate is smooth and rounded to avoid damage to the fishes' mouths.

This large plant, a variety of Java fern, draws attention away from the rocky theme.

Big fish

Some of the larger fish available in the trade really do need big tanks with plenty of space. Fish such as the Quetzal cichlid *(Theraps synspilus)* will reach up to 40cm (16in) in an aquarium, but if housed correctly, make an excellent display fish. One of the most popular big cichlids is the Jack Dempsey *(Cichlasoma octofasciatum)*. It has lovely markings, but adult males can be quite aggressive. Another brightly coloured fish is the Nicaragua cichlid *(Cichlasoma nicaraguense)*, which will grow to 25cm (10in). The Jaguar cichlid *(Nandopsis managuensis)* is best described as a beautifully evil-looking fish. When adult, it is one of the most stunning fish available, but

A heater guard is essential in this display to protect the heater from the fish or falling rockwork.

Position large rocks to create caves and hiding places that the fish may use for breeding

at a size of up to 50cm (20in), it is also quite a handful. Other large species include *Amphilophus labiatus* (the red devil) and *Nandopsis umbriferus* (the blue-flecked cichlid).

Little fish

A well-known Central American cichlid is the firemouth cichlid *(Cichlasoma meeki)*. It grows to just 15cm (6in) and is relatively peaceful. Groups of *C. meeki* can be kept together with few behavioural problems, but when they breed they become very defensive and aggressive. Their common name comes from the bright red coloration that develops around the mouth and gills. Firemouths are able to inflate their throat and gills as an act of aggression. Amazingly, this fish is sometimes sold as a community fish.

The convict cichlid *(Cichlasoma nigrofasciatum)* is so-called because of its striped patterning. It will breed easily in the aquarium, preferably in a cave. Other suitable small Central American cichlids (up to 15cm/6in) include *Cichlasoma salvini,* *C. spilurum* and *Herotilapia multispinosa* (the rainbow cichlid).

Catfish

Generally speaking, the larger cichlids will ignore most catfish, providing the catfish keep to themselves. However, when dealing with fish such as these cichlids, it is always best to be cautious. If you do wish to add any catfish or algae-eaters, then stick to large fish that can handle themselves, such as the suckermouth catfish or plecostomus (Loricariidae family).

Below: The Jack Dempsey cichlid (Cichlasoma octofasciatum) *is a favourite aquarium fish among many aquarists. This is one of the most aggressive and attractive Central American cichlids.*

Above: Often sold as 'plecostomus', this fish (Pterygoplichthys sp.), is an excellent algae eater and robust enough to mix with Central American cichlids.

Controlling aggression

Due to the nature of these cichlids, it is important to stock the aquarium correctly to avoid any unnecessary harm or death. The first thing to note is that there are no methods of altering the natural aggression or behaviour of these fish. Crowding methods, such as those recommended for Lake Malawi cichlids will not work; you simply end up with one dominant fish that terrorizes all the other inhabitants. The only sensible approach is to allow the fish plenty of room, use the largest aquarium you can and stock as few fish as possible. Decide which fish you would like to keep first and make sure that they are all of similar sizes, both when they are first introduced and when fully grown. If you add to your stock over a period of time, it is a good idea to move the decor around each time you introduce a new fish. This will eliminate any territories that may have already been formed.

Right: In the right environment, the Nicaragua cichlid (Cichlasoma nicaraguense) *develops a beautiful coloration, which is often brighter in females than males. The striking dark line may fade with age.*

An Australian River

Australia is home to a wide range of ecosystems, from tropical rainforests to vast open desert. Throughout all these habitats, there are rivers, pools and waterholes that are home to some interesting and little-known fish species.

Sweeping river homes

Australian rivers and the pools, streams and springs alongside are home to a wide range of hardy and adaptable fish.

Several river systems run across the Australian continent, including the Murry-Darling system, the fifth largest in the world. Despite this, there are relatively few Australian freshwater fish species compared with other river systems. Even fewer of these are popular aquarium fish; the only well-known freshwater Australian fishes are the rainbowfish family and only a few of these are actually from Australia!

Given the nature of the landscape, there are many unexplored watery habitats throughout Australia, indicating that there are also many undiscovered fish species. Some pools and waterways are only temporary – drying up and disappearing – but if created by flooding, they frequently contain many fish species. Many fish also breed during the floods, so any new habitats created often contain a young population of fish.

Above: The banded rainbowfish (Melanotaenia trifasciata) *is a true native Australian rainbowfish. This specimen is young and has yet to develop its full coloration and body shape.*

Rain in the hills

In high areas, the river cuts through the undulating landscape and contains many spectacular waterfalls and pools that are a haven for isolated groups of fish. In tropical climates, the rivers experience heavy monsoon rains during the summer months. This vast influx of water creates new paths through the landscape and extensive flooding of existing river systems. Further down the river, in low-lying areas, the riverbed is sandy and the banks are shallow, almost like a continuous series of beaches.

Fallen trees

Many of the tributaries of the Murry River are full of fallen trees and wood debris, providing a maze of underwater forest and an excellent habitat for fish. Large carnivorous predators patrol the open waters searching for a meal. The fallen vegetation offers a place of safety for smaller fish, which can be found here in large numbers.

Tough little guys

Because of the constantly changing habitats caused by flooding, isolated pools and dry seasons, the fish of Australia can cope with a wide range of environmental conditions. Virtually all the Australian fish can live in temperatures ranging from 15 to 35°C (59 to 95°F). Many can cope with even wider ranges, and the desert goby *(Chlamydogobius eremius)* is said to survive in waters that may reach extremes of between 4 and 42°C (39 and 104°F) for short periods of time. Many habitats are also brackish and can rapidly fluctuate in salinity. Australian fish can survive almost instantaneous changes in salinity of up to 15ppt (parts per thousand). This level is nearly 50% the strength of sea-water. This evolved indestructibility means that Australian species are ideal for the aquarium and will adapt to a wide range of conditions.

The substrate

Virtually all the habitats of Australian waterways are either carved out of rock or sandy-bottomed rivers and pools. Silver sand is the obvious and best choice for this aquarium substrate. Lime-free gravel will achieve a similar effect or you can use dedicated layered planting substrates (see page 27).

Rockwork

Rocks are not a major part of this display, but we have used two large pieces of slate here as a contrast to the other decor. For the best effect in this design, partially hide them with plants and wood so that only the top half is visible. Any type of inert rock can be used in this aquarium. We have also placed a few flat, rounded rocks in the substrate, as if the water flow had partly exposed them.

Use wood in this aquarium to imitate tree roots emerging from the river bed or bank.

You can achieve an interesting effect in this display by using rocks to create an impression of the flow of the river. This can be done by banking up sand on one side of a rock, as if it had been pushed there by water movement and creating a small dip in the substrate on the other side where natural water movement would move the sand.

Wood

The wood used in this aquarium simulates the fallen branches of trees. If you are feeling adventurous, you could try fixing or hanging roots or

This large Amazon sword plant (Echinodorus *sp.*) *makes an excellent 'river bank' plant.*

This Sagittaria *sp. is a superb foreground plant that will spread.*

branchlike pieces of wood from the top of the aquarium, but make sure that the pieces do not all reach the tank floor. This will help create the illusion of vegetation coming in from above the water surface.

Plants

Virtually all the plants here are from various American or African environments. The large Amazon swords *(Echinodorus* sp.*)* are ideal 'river bank' plants, and grouped like this they offer cover and protection for small fish that will swim among the stalks and leaves. As low-growing foreground plants, we have used various *Cryptocoryne*

Cryptocoryne sp. are hardy plants that can be separated and spread across the foreground.

and *Sagittaria* species. They will remain small and spread across the aquarium floor, where the fish will enjoy foraging among them. Adopt a random approach with the planting here, as it would be in nature.

The fish

The range of Australian fish found in the hobby is rather limited to say the least, but a few interesting fish are available. Many of the well-known rainbowfish family are not actually from Australia but make excellent additions to this type of display.

Bottom dwellers

There are a number of bottom-dwelling fish throughout Australia. The most common ornamental fish is the shark catfish, or Berney's shark cat, *(Hexanematichthys graeffei).* This is a relatively peaceful, daylight-active shoaling catfish. It can reach sizes up to 25cm (10in), which may be too big for this small community. The desert goby, in contrast, will grow no bigger than 6cm (2.4in) and spend its time darting around the substrate. Provide it with plenty of hiding places so that it feels safe and confident in the aquarium. It is a peaceful fish, although males are territorial and will fight. A number of gobies are found in Australian waters but very few are available as ornamental fish.

Gudgeon

The gudgeon family (Eleotrididae) constitute a wide-ranging part of the Australian fish fauna, ranging in size from just 4cm (1.6in) to over 40cm (16in). They can be found around roots and vegetation, resting or swimming in midwater. Gudgeon are often sold as coldwater fish, although many live happily in tropical waters and most will grow no bigger than 10cm (4in). True Australian gudgeon may be hard to obtain but can be substituted with non-native species.

Rainbowfish

These are the most commonly known group of Australian fishes. Several varieties are available in the hobby, although many of them are

The Australian river aquarium

This Amazon sword (Echinodorus sp.) is a large plant that creates a striking background in the aquarium.

These large slate rocks make a bold statement in the display.

Cryptocoryne sp. make excellent foreground plants. They will thrive in the sandy substrate.

The wood here provides a small cave to which fish can retreat.

from New Guinea rather than Australia. Their availability can be attributed to their stunning coloration, peaceful nature and ease of keeping. Rainbowfish are found in a wide variety of habitats throughout Australia, usually in large groups around vegetation or other debris. They are a valuable source of food for large predatory fishes, as well as many birds. They also help to control mosquito populations in the wild by feeding off the larvae. Native Australian rainbowfish include *Melanotaenia fluviatilis*, *M. trifasciata* and *M. splendida*.

Alien fish

A number of fish have been introduced into Australian waters by

You can separate clumps of Sagittaria *sp. into smaller plants and spread them across the foreground.*

A Java fern (Microsorium pteropus) *glows in the spotlight.*

various means, often by irresponsible fishkeepers. Although they are not native fishes, they do live and breed in Australian waters. They include mosquitofish *(Gambusia affinis)*, mollies and guppies *(Poecilia sp.)*, platies and swordtails *(Xiphophorus sp.)*, goldfish *(Carassius auratus)* and rosy barbs *(Barbus conchonius)*.

Right: Gobio gobio *can represent the Gudgeon family in this aquarium. It spends its time on the aquarium floor and patrolling the aquarium.*

Below: When fully coloured, the bosemani rainbowfish (Melanotaenia bosemani) *is more akin to many marine fish than any freshwater species.*

The dangers of introducing alien species

An alien species is one that is not native to an area but has been introduced and manages to survive, breed and sustain a population. Alien species can cause a lot of damage to the ecosystems they are introduced to, competing for food, killing native species, destroying the surrounding environment and generally upsetting nature's balance. Many alien fish species are found not only in Australia but worldwide. As a result, many fish species are restricted and even banned in some countries, making it hard for fishkeepers to obtain fish that may survive in native waters. It is vital that fishkeepers behave responsibly and never release fish into the wild. The fish shown here are *Barbus ticto*.

A European River

In temperate climates, the underwater habitat is far less luxurious than in the tropics, but no less interesting. These rivers and streams are home to a wide range of colourful fishes that are a joy to keep and observe in the aquarium.

Fish from European habitats are often overlooked or ignored as ornamental fish because of the vast array of tropical fish available. This is a great shame, as many European fish are suitable for the aquarium and provide a constant source of fascination for their owners.

Fish eat fish world...
One of the factors that makes European fish interesting is their feeding behaviour. Many small fish feed on invertebrates, such as molluscs, crustaceans and insect

Something different
European rivers, pools and streams are home to some familiar fish species whose behaviour and personality earn them a place in the aquarium.

larvae, which are readily available in the substrate or in open water. A favourite food for smaller fish are insects caught at the water surface. Other small fish feed on tiny animals found in the substrate or on plankton in the open waters. Larger fish from these rivers are often carnivorous, feeding on a wide variety of prey, including other fish. The best-known example of this type of fish is the pike. This predator will sit amongst tree roots or vegetation virtually motionless and perfectly camouflaged for long periods of time, waiting for a meal to arrive. As soon as a likely candidate arrives, the pike slowly turns, unnoticed, until it is facing its prey, then swiftly opens its wide mouth, sucking in its prey before clamping its sharp teeth around the ill-fated victim.

Just to be different

Most native European fishes breed in a similar manner. When a pair is established and ready to breed, the female will lay her eggs and attach them to stones, plants, wood or the riverbed. The male then discharges milt (sperm) to fertilize them. Fish that lay few eggs make some effort to look after their young. In the case of sticklebacks (Gasterosteidae family),

it is the male who does most of the work. Initially, a male who is ready to breed will choose a suitable site and create a 'nest' from plant material and a specially created cementing substance. When the nest is ready, the male may breed with several females, with the eggs being laid and fertilized in the nest. The male then guards the eggs and the young for a short time.

Bitterling *(Rhodeus sericeus amarus)* have a very unusual way of protecting their developing eggs and young. When breeding, the female grows a long tubelike structure called an ovipositor for egglaying. This tube can measure over 4cm (1.6in). She quickly inserts the ovipositor

Below: The three-spined stickleback (Gasterosteus aculeatus) *can be found throughout Europe and many fishkeepers have started their hobby by collecting and keeping this interesting little fish.*

into the breathing opening of a swan or freshwater mussel, where an egg is laid and then fertilized by the male. The young develop and grow inside the mussel before being released up to four weeks later.

Time to rest

During the winter months, water temperatures drop steadily, often to below 0°C (32°F). Fish cope with this by drastically reducing their metabolism and entering a state bordering on hibernation. During this time, they can be found under banks or vegetation near the riverbed, where temperatures are highest. They feed very rarely and waste little energy.

The substrate

The natural substrate of this biotope would depend on the exact area being represented. Generally speaking, either pea gravel or sand would be satisfactory. We have used silver sand here due to its supportive nature and because it contrasts with the rocks and stones in the display.

The rockwork

The boulders in this display represent the weathered, rounded rocks found in many European river systems. Smaller rocks, pebbles and some pea gravel help to recreate accurately the

Small pebbles can be scattered across the aquarium floor.

effect of a natural river bed. In many areas of the natural habitat, the flow of the river will remove any topsoil or sediment to expose the underlying rocks. Piling the pebbles and stones into groups around pieces of wood and larger rocks imitates the natural grouping that occurs as a result of water flow moving small pebbles downstream until they are caught against a larger object.

Wood

Here, a few pieces of bogwood represent tree roots exposed by the erosion of the river's flow. Place the wood at the rear of the aquarium as a background or partly bury it in the substrate as if it were

Once established, this piece of false wood will become indistinguishable from the real thing.

Elodea canadensis *is an excellent and hardy coldwater plant.*

continuing underground. The large piece in the middle of this display is synthetic but fits in with the rest of the decor.

The plants

There are a number of coldwater plants available that would be suited to this display. In nature, most areas of the river are not heavily planted so we have only used two species in this tank. Some floating plants introduce an extra element to the display. Suitable plants for a European river biotope would include *Elodea* sp., *Egeria* sp., *Fontinalis antipyretica* (willow moss), *Lysimachia nummularia* (creeping Jenny), *Lemna* sp., *Ceratophyllum demersum* (hornwort), and some *Myriophyllum* species.

Keep it cool

Some of the fish suited to this display will not be able to cope with high temperatures. Bear in mind that the temperature can rise to quite high levels, even in an unheated indoor aquarium. Make sure that the tank is not situated in direct sunlight or in any position where it is exposed to unwanted heat. Good ventilation helps to reduce rising temperatures.

The fish

Despite the slightly more conservative coloration of coldwater fishes compared to their tropical counterparts, many European fishes are of unique interest to the fishkeeper. The most interesting fish due to its breeding habits is the bitterling *(Rhodeus sericeus amarus,* see page 78*).* This peaceful fish is

Hornwort (Ceratophyllum demersum) *is commonly available as a pond plant.*

ideal for a community aquarium. The males are beautifully coloured, especially when breeding, with a blue, green and red iridescent sheen.

Substrate dwellers

The most commonly available bottom-dwelling fish is the weather loach *(Misgurnus fossilis)*. This long, cylindrical fish can grow quite large (up to 30cm/12in) so it will need a reasonably sized aquarium. Its common name is the result of its restless behaviour and habit of taking gulps of air when the atmospheric pressure changes, a sign of an oncoming change in the weather.

Another attractive bottom-dweller is the gudgeon *(Gobio gobio)*. It will grow no bigger than 20cm (8in). A

The European river aquarium

Use plants sparingly in this display. This is Elodea canadensis.

These large boulders are major features of the aquarium and can be surrounded with smaller items of decor.

Blend small pea gravel into the substrate.

Rounded stones and cobbles simulate natural weathering.

fish that is often available is the sterlet *(Acipenser ruthenus)*, along with other sturgeon *(Acipenser* sp.). They are peaceful fish, but often unsuitable for aquariums as they can reach lengths of up to 1m (39in).

Midwater swimmers

For the midwater ranges, an ideal inhabitant is the minnow *(Phoxinus phoxinus)*. This peaceful little fish will be quite happy in the aquarium and grow no bigger than 10cm (4in). The minnow is ideally suited to this aquarium. In the wild it can be found in clear streams and rivers with sandy or stony beds. Minnows are shoaling fish, so keep them in groups of four or more in the tank to make them feel at home.

Placing wood partly in the substrate imitates uncovered roots.

Hornwort (Ceratophyllum demersum) *will grow quickly. You can take cuttings and replant them.*

Fill gaps between larger rocks with small pebbles.

Sticklebacks (Gasterosteidae family) make ideal companions for the minnow. They are similar in size and spend their time either swimming in midwater or foraging around the plants and substrate.

Sunfish (Centrarchidae family) are often available to fishkeepers. The most common is the pumpkinseed *(Lepomis gibbosus)*. It originated in North America, but was introduced into Europe in the 1890s. Normally, the pumpkinseed is a peaceful, attractively coloured fish, but during the breeding season it can become territorial and aggressive.

The one and only

Of course, there is one other fish that can be included in this setup, namely the common goldfish *(Carassius auratus)*. It is ideally suited to the aquarium and can withstand a wide range of water conditions. Unfortunately, it is the fish's own hardy nature that has allowed it to become one of the most abused fish in the aquarium hobby. Goldfish require exactly the same care as any other fish and should not be neglected, as they often are. Remember, too, that with the proper attention, goldfish can easily grow up to 35cm (14in) in length.

Right: The hardy pumpkinseed (Lepomis gibbosus) *will tolerate a wide range of temperatures and will will grow up to 20cm (8in) long in the aquarium.*

Below: The bitterling (Rhodeus sericeus amarus) *is a common favourite in any coldwater aquarium. Its iridescent coloration rivals many tropical fish.*

Right: The minnow (Phoxinus phoxinus) is a small fish that will swim in the middle and surface levels of the aquarium. It has an excellent sense of smell and hearing.

A FLOODED FOREST

During the rainy season in the Amazon there comes a point when the river can no longer hold the massive influx of water. It bursts its banks and spreads over a wide expanse, creating a whole new world for its aquatic inhabitants.

A watery world

The igapó, or flooded forest, is an annual event in the Amazon, where flooding can last up to 10 months depending on the severity of rainfall.

Generally speaking, the seasonal floods will last for about six months of the year. In this time, vast areas covering in total over 100,000 square kilometres (39,000 sq miles) of the forest are flooded in water, in some places as deep as 10m (33ft).

Fry food
In midwinter, water levels begin to rise rapidly, marking the arrival of the floods. Small shoaling fish, such as many tetras, will have recently spawned in the riverbanks. The influx of vegetation and leaves will be broken down by small detritus feeders, which in turn become a plentiful source of food for fry.

Sweet smells
Most fish in these areas of the Amazon will feed on fruits and seeds from the surrounding forest. During this period of flooding, these foods

are available in quantity. The fish in the flooded forest have evolved a keen sense of smell that allows them to identify individual species of trees that harbour the best fruits. Trees that are about to drop fruits and seeds will exhibit slight biochemical changes that fish will target.

Bug hunting
Larger fish also inhabit these areas. Pacus and silver dollars feed on fruits and seeds, cruising through the trees in search of food. The arrowana, measuring up to 1m (39in), is one of the largest fish in the world to feed on insects and spiders. It can see both in and out of the water at the same time, allowing it to spot falling insects before they even hit the surface. Arrowanas will also jump out of water to catch prey on branches; fully grown specimens will even try to capture birds and bats.

Food fish
Of course, there are other predators in and around the waters. Large shoals of piranha search for a meal of other fish and animals. River turtles also hunt out fish and, much like the piranhas, can easily take large chunks out of any fish they pass.

Jaguar also live in the forest and they are accomplished fish-catchers. They will rest on tree branches above the water and imitate falling fruits by gently splashing the water surface. This attracts fish that swim to the surface to take the imaginary fruits. At this point the jaguar will roll off the branch onto its prey and drag its meal to the shore.

Heading home
As the water levels start to decline, the aquatic occupants will head back to the main river or towards one of the many pools and channels formed by the undulating landscape. A few aquatic animals, such as some bivalve mussels and sponges, will not leave the flooded forest. Instead, when the water is gone, they will have entered a dormant state, preserving energy until the rains come again the following year.

Substrate
In the flooded forest the natural substrate would be a mixture of sands and mud. Mud is obviously not an option, so use silver sand

Use black gravel to darken the aquarium floor.

Planting substrate will imitate natural muck and mulm.

covered with a sprinkling of peat or a planting substrate sold specifically for aquarium use to recreate the desired effect. Use as little peat or planting substrate as possible, as it will cloud the water. Adding some darker gravel or even crushed and washed coal also adds to the mood.

Wood

Select pieces of bogwood that look like fallen or broken branches and place them in the middle of the planting areas. You can wash or soak bogwood before using it to remove tannic acids. However, in this kind of display, a slight brown tinge to the water can add to the overall effect.

You may wish to add some large pieces of bogwood to represent tree roots. If you can find a piece with a suitably large shape and rounded diameter, it is a very good idea. Plant a few smaller plants around the base of the 'tree' and it will soon become a major feature in the aquarium.

Cryptocorynes are good foreground plants.

Plants

In this design there are two clear planting areas, one at the surface and one on the substrate. If possible, it is best to keep the two separate and allow swimming space inbetween. The plants at the bottom of the aquarium should be low-growing foreground plants or ones that can be easily trimmed back. Use plants such as *Sagittaria* sp. to make grasslike outcrops. You can create a small bushy effect using small *Heteranthera zosterifolia,* which

As bark will float, this piece was siliconed to a piece of glass, placed on the aquarium floor and held down by the substrate.

can be trimmed back regularly. Plants with twiglike stalks and a terrestrial appearance, such as any of the *Hygrophila* species, will give the impression of flooded land plants.

Cover the surface with floating plants, such as water lettuce *(Pistia stratiotes)* and water hyacinth *(Eichhornia crassipes),* which will produce massive roots that provide protection for the fish. You may prefer not to use floating plants, because they may not thrive if your aquarium has an enclosed lid. This is no problem; many areas of the flooded forest have calm, uninterrupted surfaces. If you do not use floating plants you may wish to break up this 'empty' space by hanging some suitable plastic plants or twigs into the water from above to represent the overhanging foliage.

It is possible to obtain terrestrial plants from areas that often flood, such as the habitat we are recreating. These include *Acorus* sp. (Japanese rush), *Ophiopogon* sp. (fountain plant), *Dracaena* sp. (dragon plant) and *Syngonium podophyllum* (stardust ivy). These plants will live underwater for a limited time that varies with each plant. If they start to die off, take them out of the water and grow them terrestrially for a short while.

This synthetic plant represents overhanging foliage.

The fish

The flooded forest is home to any of the fish normally found in the affected rivers and tributaries. In the aquarium we can only house a handful of these species. Many of the larger fish, such as the pacus *(Colossoma* sp. and *Myletes* sp.),* piranhas *(Serrasalmus* sp.)* and arrowanas *(Osteoglossum* sp.),* will

Alternanthera reineckii adds a subtle hint of colour.

83

be unmanageable and destructive in most aquariums. As this biotope aquarium is quite heavily planted, limit the inhabitants to smaller, more peaceful fish that will not damage the display. Many of the more suitable fish for this display also mirror the inhabitants of the Amazon acid pool setup described on pages 88-95.

The flooded forest aquarium

Shoaling fish

Small shoaling fish, such as many tetras, will be quite at home in this environment. The planting, both on the aquarium floor and from above, provides plenty of safe retreats and will give them a strong sense of security. One of the most commonly known tetras is the cardinal tetra *(Paracheirodon axelrodi)*. This

The main 'object' in this aquarium is a line of bark across the centre. It is actually a number of small pieces joined together, creating the effect of a larger but fragmented whole.

Floating plants, such as Pistia stratiotes, *help to block out excessive light and provide a retreat for fishes.*

popular fish is readily available and to the untrained eye is almost identical to the neon tetra. However, the cardinal's coloration is enhanced by the red and blue bars extending along the whole body. A less brightly coloured but no less stunning fish for this tank is the black widow tetra *(Gymnocorymbus ternetzi)*. The dark colour of this active and interesting species allows it to disappear into the background at will. The black widow is one of the hardier varieties; it will live happily in a wide range of water conditions.

If you regularly monitor the water quality of your aquarium and provide a low pH, acid environment, then the rummy-nose tetra *(Hemigrammus bleheri)* is a must-

Some synthetic plants positioned in the top righthand corner of the aquarium simulate overhanging branches.

The gaps and caves created by the wood are great hiding places for catfish and small tetras.

This Echinodorus sp. is a specimen plant. Use only a single plant in an aquarium of this size.

The silver sand is sprinkled with darker substrates to keep the dark feel of the aquarium.

Left: The rummy-nose tetra (Hemigrammus bleheri) *has striking coloration on the head, which will improve with correct care and attention to water quality. This fish will shoal in tight groups and swim amongst the plants.*

Right: The aptly named black widow tetra, Gymnocorymbus ternetzi, *has a dark and sombre coloration, but is a hardy and highly attractive fish. With age, the body colour may fade to dark grey.*

have. In the right conditions, this small, peaceful fish will develop truly stunning coloration and become a welcome addition to the display.

Specimen fish
If ever there were two fish made for this display, they would without a doubt be the altum angelfish *(Pterophyllum altum)* and discus *(Symphysodon sp.).* The altum angel is a rare variety of the angelfish, with a taller body and steeply rising head.

The discus is a beautiful and elegant fish, often referred to as the king of aquarium fish due to its regal appearance and because so many fishkeepers aspire to keep it successfully. However, only experienced fishkeepers should keep discus, as they require perfect water conditions and a great deal of care. Both discus and altum angels are peaceful and, if raised together from young, will form a close-knit group within the aquarium.

A FLOODED FOREST

Surface patrol

One of the most unusual-looking groups of fish available in the hobby are the hatchetfishes (Gasteropelecidae family). Their unusual shape is the result of the massive muscles of the pectoral fins, which allow the fish literally to take off above the water surface and thus avoid predators in their natural environment. Hatchetfish stay at the surface of the aquarium, constantly looking for food. Living near the surface, they will appreciate floating plants as a means of protection. If

Below: The Farlowella group of catfish use their twiglike body shape as effective camouflage. In the aquarium, they will spend their (often shortlived) time resting on wood or feeding from algae.

you keep them, be sure to cover the aquarium, as they will often jump from the surface.

Catfish sticks

Even more bizarre than the hatchetfish is the Farlowella group of catfish. They look exactly like sticks and will be hidden in the aquarium. They are shy and timid, but given the right environment their confidence will grow. They are naturally found in floodplains and bogs and may only live for a short time due to their seasonal nature. These algae-eaters hardly ever seem to move in the aquarium; even when touched they will not stir, but keep up the convincing stick impression. These are fascinating creatures for those who will appreciate them.

AN AMAZON ACID POOL

After the rains have gone and the flooded forest returns to normal, many large pools of water remain as a reminder of the floods. Most of these pools dry up and any inhabitants will become a source of food for the forest animals.

As the pool floor was previously terrestrial, there is a mass of organic matter that will die off and begin to alter the chemistry of the pool. The dissolved organic matter and humic acid released from the rotting vegetation will reduce the pH levels in the pool to as low as 4 or 5. The water will quickly become stained by the tannic acids and change to a dark, tealike brown colour. While the pH levels are unacceptable to many fish, a few will find these conditions ideal. And for some fish they are a trigger to begin breeding.

Living pools

Some pools will be large enough to sustain themselves and will continue to be home to a wide range of aquatic creatures.

Baby food

Some of these acid pools are in areas devoid of cover from overhanging vegetation and receive unfiltered direct sunlight. As the pool is a self-contained body, the sunlight will quickly heat the water to unusually high temperatures, often greater than 33°C (93°F). The combination of

Left: The angelfish (Pterophyllum scalare) *can be found living and breeding in Amazon pools. In the aquarium they make magnificent specimen fish and, given the right environment, are easy to breed.*

low pH levels and high water temperatures will stimulate fish such as discus to breed. This environment is ideal for the raising of young fry. The pool's high organic load results in a slight stagnation that allows blooms of microalgae and infusoria to form. These are an abundant form of suitable food for tiny fry. The availability of large amounts of food and relatively few predators mean that the fry's survival chances are greatly increased.

Hiding and hunting

The nutrient-rich waters and low oxygen levels of the acid pool are also ideal for plants to thrive in. Both aquatic and some semi-terrestrial plants will grow in blooms beneath the surface. Sometimes the conditions are too extreme even for plants to grow in, so numbers are limited. The pool floor is scattered with roots and branches from the surrounding forest and these lie on a substrate of

sediment and nutrient-rich soil. The plants and debris scattered across the pool floor provide hiding places and hunting grounds both for the larger fish and the young fry. Many small aquatic animals can be found here, feeding off the detritus.

The substrate

The natural substrate of the acid pool is much the same as that of the flooded forest and consists of mud and sediment. Once again, use silver sand as a replacement in the aquarium or, alternatively, add fine,

These red chippings complement the colours of the aquarium.

lime-free gravel. This layer can be diffused slightly by sprinkling or scattering varying grades of darker substrates over the surface. In this aquarium, we have used a gravel with a natural reddish colour, which helps to enhance the dark, earthy feel of the tank. If you do use alternative substrates, try to keep to subtle shades of 'autumn' colours, such as brown, black and red.

Wood

Adding natural-style bogwood to an aquarium, as opposed to precleaned or manufactured wood, will stain the water and alter its colour. In many tanks, this is an undesirable state of affairs, but in this setup it positively helps to create an atmosphere. The placing of wood can be entirely random, as long as it is aesthetically pleasing. Select pieces that either look like tree roots, with one or both ends buried in the substrate, or that resemble randomly placed broken branches and debris.

Plants such as this Anubias *sp. have a distinct and attractive leaf shape.*

Planting

Place plants such as *Anubias* sp. along the pieces of wood. If you 'wedge' them into cracks in the wood, they will soon root and eventually spread. The two main grouped plants here are *Heteranthera zosterifolia* and *Hygrophila* sp. but many other plants could be included to the same effect. Place the

The tannic acids produced by bogwood will stain the water and help to lower pH levels – ideal for the acid pool environment.

occasional smaller plant along the aquarium floor. We have used some dwarf Amazon swordplants. For some of the more timid fish that may be kept in this type of aquarium, floating plants offer a source of shade and protection. Water lettuce *(Pistia stratiotes)* is ideal, as it produces roots that are attractive and functional but not too long. Other floating plants, such as *Azolla* sp., *Salvinia* sp. and *Riccia* sp. are also suitable. If you are creating an aquarium with accurate location species, you can also add some suitable terrestrial plants. Those able to tolerate being underwater for long periods of time would naturally be found in pools such as these.

Special notes

If you plan to recreate the conditions as they would be in nature, you will need to make some alterations to the

The stems of hygrophila provide hiding places for small fish, while larger fish find cover underneath the leaves.

Water lettuce (Pistia stratiotes) *will float on the surface and produce trailing roots, breaking up the light and providing protection for fish.*

water chemistry. To obtain the low hardness and acidic conditions, either use a proprietary treatment or specially prepared reverse osmosis water. Bear in mind that when you stock the aquarium, the fish you buy are unlikely to have been housed in these conditions. In this case, you may need to acclimatize them slowly in a separate aquarium before introducing them to the main tank.

The fish

A wide range of fish can be found in the acid pools just after the floods have raised the water level.

The undulating forest landscape ensures that many fish are cut off from the main river when the waters begin to recede. In this event, fish are 'herded' into the pools, many of which will dry out, causing the fish to die. Of the fish that survive, only a few will be able to tolerate and live comfortably in the harsh conditions of the acid pool environment.

Discus and angelfish

One fish that lives in these conditions is the discus (*Symphysodon sp.*), which finds the low pH and hardness levels ideal. Discus will grow to over 20cm (8in), so you will need a reasonably sized aquarium to keep a group of these fish. Discus are some of the most difficult tropical freshwater fish to keep, because they

The Amazon acid pool aquarium

Water lettuce (Pistia stratiotes) *will rapidly multiply in the right conditions, creating a cover of roots and leaves and breaking up any light entering the aquarium.*

This Hygrophila *sp. offers protection for fish of all sizes.*

These red chippings add colour to the sandy floor and combine well with the wood-stained water.

Bogwood pieces will stain and soften the water, as well as representing tree debris.

demand impeccable water quality and water conditions. The popular angelfish *(Pterophyllum scalare)* is found together with discus in the wild. Like the discus, the angel is a wonderfully majestic fish that will complement this design of aquarium perfectly. Both fish belong to the cichlid family, but unlike many of their relatives, they are peaceful in the aquarium and will form close bonds with their tankmates if raised in groups. In the right conditions, both discus and angelfish may form pairs and even breed.

Shoaling tetras
The group of small characin fish commonly known as tetras are also perfectly suited to the conditions in

Plants such as Anubias sp. *can be grown out of the bogwood and create unexpected foliage in the centre of the display.*

Use one or two dense groups of plants in brighter areas. This Heteranthera zosterifolia *can be trimmed to varying sizes, accentuating its bushlike appearance.*

the acid pool. These small shoaling fish should be kept in groups of six or more. By keeping them in groups as they would be in nature, they will feel far more comfortable and confident in the aquarium, and this will be reflected in their health and colour. In the wild, these fish dart in and out of vegetation and debris, hunting tiny aquatic creatures and any small fruits or seeds shed by the forest vegetation.

Bottom-dwellers

Catfish can also be found in the acid waters, feeding on small aquatic insects and animals on the muddy pool floor. Because of the high levels of rotting vegetation and organic matter in the pools, there is an abundance of detritus-feeding organisms in the substrate – an ideal food source for some catfish. Catfish such as *Hoplosternum* sp. make ideal specimens for the larger aquarium, while a shoal of *Corydoras* sp. would suit a smaller one. Although in nature the corydoras group of catfish are found mainly in vegetated flowing waters, they occur in almost all stretches of water in the Amazon and would be at home in this setup.

Corydoras catfish, like the tetras, are shoaling fish by nature, so keep them this way in the aquarium. There are many different varieties of corydoras available to the hobbyist and they will all shoal together quite happily, so you can 'mix and match' different species to form a shoal.

Below: This Hoplosternum thoracatum *will forage amongst the plants and substrate for any waste food, thus performing an important 'cleaning' function within the aquarium.*

Above: *The discus* (Symphysodon *sp.*)
demands dedicated care and attention in
the aquarium, but will reward such care
with stunning coloration and beauty.

95

A SOUTHEAST ASIAN SWAMP

The swamps of Southeast Asia could be described as an underwater jungle. Dense aquatic foliage covers every available space, creating a habitat for small labyrinth fish and rasboras. An ideal setting to recreate in the aquarium.

Swamp creatures

The numerous swamps, pools and irrigation channels are densely packed with aquatic plants that provide food and protection for wildlife.

The abundance of vegetation in the Southeast Asian swamp creates a habitat that is unique and unparalleled. The muddy, nutrient-rich substrate is ideal for plants to root in and the slow-moving waters allow the vegetation to spread in dense groups. Beneath the water, plants spread into every available space in a bushlike fashion and rapidly grow towards the surface in the competition for sunlight. This surface growth often leaves open space in the lower areas, where the light is too dim for plants to produce foliage. The water surface is also covered with a mass of floating plants that quickly block out light to the underwater habitat, creating a dark and murky atmosphere that the fish will enjoy. Along the banks and shallows, masses of reeds and bamboo thrive in the wet and tropical environment. Moving onto

Left: The dwarf gourami (Colisa lalia) is now available in many colour morphs. This beautiful red male fish will add colour to any aquarium. Take special care with these fish as they are intolerant of bad water quality and susceptible to bacterial infections.

the land, the shallows are shaded by a wealth of tropical trees.

Blame it on the plants

All this vegetation does have its drawbacks and the fish in this environment have had to adapt to extreme water conditions created by the abundance of vegetation and the nutrient-rich waters. The large amount of organic matter and living plants use up many minerals in the water and through respiration release vast quantities of CO_2 (carbon dioxide). The lack of mineral content reduces the natural hardness in the swamps to only a few degrees. The introduction of CO_2 and humic acids from dead vegetation creates very acid conditions and without any hardness to act as a buffer, the pH can fluctuate dramatically throughout the day. It is quite common to find a pH of 5 or even lower in this environment.

Take a deep breath

The dense vegetation almost eliminates any water movement within these habitats. Between

February and October, the air temperature rises and with little depth and movement, the water heats quickly, rising to an average of 28°C (82°F). The combination of high temperatures, dense planting, high organic load and lack of water movement means that oxygen levels can become very low, especially at night when the plants stop photosynthesizing. Although many plants will enjoy the low oxygen environment, it can be a big problem for the fish, which have to find ways of adapting to these extreme environmental conditions.

The substrate

A substrate of fine silver sand will be suitable, both as a general planting medium and to recreate the natural substrate. A few pebbles and a fine sprinkling of pea gravel add extra interest. Because there are so many plants in this setup, it is worth putting some extra effort into making sure that they will thrive in the aquarium. Ideally, tailor the substrate to the plants' requirements. You may wish to use dedicated

Cut the bamboo into various lengths for a better overall effect.

wood to recreate tree roots coming down from the banks, which can be very effective in a planted aquarium.

Bamboo canes
Bamboo is ideal in this display, both in terms of interest and for the fishes environment. To achieve a realistic effect, cut the canes into varying sizes and place the lengths randomly amongst the plants. Place some pieces singly and others in groups. Bamboo is quite light and full of air, so will float in the aquarium. To overcome this problem, silicone it to small pebbles acting as anchors. In time, bamboo will start to rot; either treat it with a suitable polyurethane varnish before putting it in the tank or replace it frequently.

Plants
The most important element of this display is the vegetation. To recreate the swamp habitat, use dense, bushy plants, such as *Heteranthera*

Lobelia cardinalis is also found in a terrestrial form and can be grown above the surface.

planting substrates, along with either silver sand, lime-free gravel or both. Adding a substrate heating cable will also benefit the plants (see page 28).

Rockwork
In fact, rocks are an unimportant aspect of this aquarium, but we have used two large ones here to help break up the dense planting. Adding large rocks to a heavily planted aquarium can help to focus attention on certain areas and makes a pleasing backdrop both to the fish and the plants.

Wood
Wood can also be used to good effect, although it is not essential for this display. It distracts attention away from the plants, creating an extra element of interest. You may wish to use

Stargrass (Heteranthera zosterifolia) can be continually trimmed to achieve a bushy effect.

This red myriophyllum (Myriophyllum mattogrossense) adds colour to the background.

zosterifolia (stargrass). To enhance the effect, trim the plants so that they are shorter towards the front of the aquarium. Tall, fine-leaved plants, such as *Cabomba* or *Myrio phyllum* sp., make a good background. These

Given adequate lighting Ludwigia repens *will produce reddish leaves.*

plants grow quickly and soon spread across the surface. Providing they do not block out too much light, this surface spread will add to the overall effect. Smaller, foreground plants, such as *Echinodorus* sp. (dwarf amazon swords), *Cryptocoryne* sp. or *Sagittaria* sp. are ideal for covering any remaining space towards the front of the aquarium. In this aquarium, we have used *Lobelia cardinalis* along almost half the foreground. This plant is often seen out of water, where it produces distinctive red flowers. In the aquarium, it is an ideal slow-growing foreground plant.

The fish
Many of the more popular fishes available in the hobby are from the swamps of Southeast Asia. In this

densely planted habitat there is little room for large fish and most inhabitants are small and peaceful. The swamp environment is full of hiding places and very little open space. The fish that live here are often timid and shy, but in the right environment they become confident and bring life and movement to the aquarium display.

Labyrinth fish

In the oxygen-depleted environment of the swamps, some of the larger inhabitants have developed a special way of taking oxygen from above the water surface. These are the labyrinth fish, so-called because of the special labyrinth organ they have developed, which can absorb oxygen from atmospheric air taken

The Southeast Asian swamp aquarium

In this aquarium, the water lettuce (Pistia stratiotes) *not only provides cover and breaks up the light, but also helps to calm the water surface and create an ideal environment for nest building.*

Cabomba *sp. make excellent background plants.*

Lobelia cardinalis *is ideal for the foreground. Its thick, rounded leaves contrast well with many of the fine bushy leaved plants.*

A few large rocks help to break up the plant-dominated display.

This Hydrocotyle *sp. is an unusual plant with an attractive yet messy appearance.*

at the water surface. Even in the aquarium, where oxygen is usually readily available, they can be seen taking gulps from the surface. The most commonly known labyrinth fish from this habitat are the gouramis, namely the pearl gourami *(Trichogaster leeri)*, the gold gourami *(T. trichopterus)* and the dwarf gourami *(Colisa lalia)*. They are all peaceful timid fish, although males will sometimes fight. The gold gourami is also available in opaline/blue and three-spot colour morphs. If you wish to keep male gold gouramis, house them in a group of at least six fish to avoid any harmful aggression.

One of the most beautiful freshwater fish in the hobby is the

Bamboo and bogwood create good focal points in this display.

Bushy plants, such as this Heteranthera sp., can be trimmed to different lengths.

Siamese fighting fish *(Betta splendens)*, which is also a labyrinth fish. Do not house this peaceful fish in a general community tank because its long fins and timid nature make it an easy target for fin-nippers or any aggressive fish. Choose its tankmates with care. It derives its common name from the vicious battles that take place between two males. If two males are housed in one tank, they will fight until one is dead.

Rasboras
The active but peaceful rasboras make an ideal addition to this setup and complement the slow-moving labyrinth fish. These small, shoaling fish swim in and out of the dense groups of plants. Although active, they will not dart around the tank

Above: *The Siamese fighting fish* (Betta splendens) *has the most attractive finnage of any tropical freshwater fish. Take special care when choosing tankmates for this striking labyrinth fish.*

and frighten other inhabitants. The most common and attractive rasbora available is the harlequin rasbora *(Rasbora heteromorpha)*. The name reflects its unusual but decorative coloration.

Down below
A number of loaches occupy the muddy floor of the swamps. These bottom-dwellers spend their time scavenging along the substrate in search of crustaceans and small aquatic creatures. The loaches from this habitat are also quite shy and timid but, given time, they should

venture out into open areas. The kuhlii loach, *Pangio kuhlii*, (also known as *Acanthophthalmus kuhlii*) is a lone fish that spends most of its time hiding, only coming out in the evenings or, in the aquarium, at feeding time. Many aquarists buy these fish, never to see them for months at a time.

Another common bottom-dweller is the clown loach *(Botia macracanthus)*, which is found in lowland waters, as well as in streams and rivers. It is a favourite with many fishkeepers, but does need proper care and good water quality. This ideal aquarium fish is often used to control snail infestations, as it readily eats any snails of a suitable size.

Below: The pearl, or lace, gourami (Trichogaster leeri) *is a hardy and peaceful fish, ideally suited to this swamp environment. Gouramis of this type and size often look best in groups.*

*Right: The harlequin rasbora (*Rasbora heteromorpha*) will contrast well with the larger gouramis. Given the added security of numerous hiding places in a heavily planted tank, these fish will shoal less tightly than normal.*

LAKE MALAWI

As the crystal clear waters of Lake Malawi lap against the rocky outcrops and sandy shores, it is hard to imagine the beautiful array of fish that swarms just beneath the surface of this vast freshwater ocean in Africa.

The cichlids of Lake Malawi are amongst the most beautifully coloured communities of fish you could hope to find in a natural freshwater habitat. In their native setting they almost seem to demand our appreciation.

Sandy, rocky, sandy...

The underwater habitats of the lake constantly alternate around the shoreline through sandy shores and rocky outcrops. It is this alternation of habitat, combined with the lake's history of rising and falling water

A special place

Lake Malawi is home to over 600 cichlid species, most of them unique to the lake. Many species occur only in certain locations within the lake.

levels, that has produced the vast diversity of fish. Many of the fish depend on the rocky outcrops for their source of food and will stick to one area, where they are part of a thriving community. Venturing out into the open waters would be dangerous, as there are many open-water predators looking for a meal.

So many fish

Over the years, the water level of the lake has fallen and risen, which has resulted in a constant rearrangement of the rocky and sandy areas. The rock-dwelling fish will move with this rearrangement, becoming divided and isolated. Once isolated, one species may become two through slight evolutionary changes. It is this process which has, over a period of time, resulted in the vast number of species in the lake today. But where is the food? At first glance it is hard to see what the fish actually feed on. In one small area, perhaps one square metre (10 square feet), there may be more than 30 fish with no apparent source of food. Vegetation is sparse and does not appear near the rocky outcrops, and there seem to be no other aquatic animals nearby. However, if you look much closer, you will see that all the rocks are covered in a dense mat of fuzzy algae. It is this 'fuzz' that houses the main source of food for the vast numbers of fish. This algal fuzz is known as 'aufwuchs' and is home to many tiny creatures that form the basis of the fishes' food. The mouths of many of the cichlids are designed to graze on the aufwuchs and consume the algae, along with any accompanying creatures. Some fish are even designed to pick out certain specific foods from the aufwuchs.

Vegetation

Due to the isolated nature of the lake, there are very few plant species. In fact, there are only about five and these include two species of

Below: Pseudotropheus zebra *can be found in many different colour morphs, depending upon which part of the lake the fish originates from.*

Silver sand is an excellent substrate for supporting rocks.

vallisneria and two species of potamogeton. The vegetation of the lake occurs close to the shore, where the lake floor is a large sandy expanse. Here, you find whole 'fields' of plants, such as *Vallisneria aethiopica*. In the clear sunlit waters, the plant grows in a compact fashion and spreads rapidly, creating a green lawn across the lake bed.

Substrate

In this aquarium we can provide the substrate exactly as it would be in nature: clean and pure sand. Once again, silver sand is the best type to use, not because it is inert but because it replicates the type of sand found in the lake itself. Sand is also an ideal base to support the weight of the rockwork. In this setup, you can see that the depth of sand is greatly increased in areas of heavy rockwork. As a general rule, make the layer of sand at least 7.5cm (3in) deep across the entire base to support heavy rockwork.

Rockwork

Most of the Malawi aquariums you see probably include lava rock as the main decor. In the lake itself there is nothing like this; boulders such as the ones we have used are the closest representation available. In fact, the rocks in the lake are identical to these boulders, the only difference being that many in the lake are much bigger. To begin with, select rocks of varying size. Here, we have used two very large boulders and graded the rest down from a medium size of about 20cm (8in) to pebbles as small as 2-3cm (0.8-1.2in). Of course, the size of rocks you decide to use depends on the size of your aquarium. For the best display, the largest rocks should be about one third to a quarter of the length of the aquarium at its widest point. In large aquariums that will be able to house larger rocks, you should make sure that the aquarium will be able to house such a weight. Put in the large rocks first, preferably fairly close to one another, and simply build up and around them with the other rocks. In nature, the rocks would lie as they had naturally fallen; try to recreate this in the aquarium. Do not try to stack rocks in columns or any unnatural formations. Finally, place smaller cobbles and pebbles randomly in any crevices created by the larger rocks. In this aquarium, we have created one area of smaller cobbles and pebbles, which helps to break up the display a little.

Safety precautions

Given the number of heavy rocks in this aquarium, take special care with both the design and construction of the tank. Make sure that it is fully supported across the entire base. This means that you should not use a stand that only supports the perimeter of the base or an aquarium that is raised by a rim around the base. Make sure you have a suitable depth of sand to support the rocks and do not use large-grade gravels, as this will concentrate pressure in one area. Do not allow any of the larger rocks to touch the glass base of the aquarium.

Although you should position the rocks in a natural fashion, so that they fully support each other, there is always a danger of falling rockwork. To avoid this risk, you may wish to carry out a 'dry run' to decide where you are going to place the rocks and then use a silicone sealant to fix them together. Apart from cracking the aquarium, any equipment is also in danger. Filtration should be via an external filter and any heaters should be protected by a heater guard or placed above the rockwork.

Alternative decor

As an alternative substrate, you may wish to use coral gravel or coral sand. This substrate contains large amounts of calcium that will raise the pH and hardness of the water. Hard water is ideal for Malawi cichlids and this type of substrate will help to 'buffer' the water and keep conditions constant. If you are unsure about using such heavy weights of rockwork or the aquarium you have is unsuitable to support such weight, then lava rock is an alternative. It is very porous and therefore contains mostly air, giving it a much lighter size to weight ratio. Although this would not be recreating the habitat precisely, it is perfectly suitable for the aquarium's inhabitants.

These large rounded stones accurately recreate the natural habitat.

The fish

The fish species of Lake Malawi are virtually all cichlids. One reason for this is that cichlids are an extremely adaptable group of fishes. The changing conditions in the lake have allowed them to adapt and survive, whilst other fish die off. The lake Malawi cichlids have also evolved to feed off the food sources in the lake.

Many have individual physical adaptations within their species that allow them to feed on certain foods.

Food for thought

Although the fish may be especially adapted to feed on one type of food, they are more likely to feed on a variety of foods. The specialized evolutionary changes in terms of

The Lake Malawi aquarium

This corner of the tank is shaded and makes a dark retreat for the aquarium's inhabitants.

The rocks provide many hiding places and territories for the cichlids.

In this aquarium, the rocks have been placed as if they had fallen into a natural pile.

A few smaller pebbles and cobbles can be used on the aquarium floor.

feeding probably occurred in times when no other food sources were easily available. If other foods are available and easier to obtain, then the fish will take them. This is why, along with a lack of 'aufwuchs' in the aquarium, these fish readily take most types of commercial food and may not be as interested in natural foods, such as algae.

Territoriality

Many of the Lake Malawi cichlids are highly aggressive and territorial. Their aggression can usually be attributed to one of three reasons. Firstly, if a fish finds a good feeding site it may defend it so that it can graze at will and keep the food for itself. Incomers will be aggressively chased away. The other main reasons

The substrate is deeper at this end of the aquarium to support the heavier rocks.

for territoriality are in the interests of successful breeding. Both sexes may defend a prospective breeding site and male aggression against other males helps to ensure that only the fittest fish will be successful in breeding. Once spawning has taken place, both the eggs and the fry are aggressively defended by the parents.

Mbuna

Cichlids can be classified into two groups: rock-dwellers, also known as 'mbuna' and sand-dwellers, or 'haps'. Most fish available for the ornamental aquarium are the mbuna. In the aquarium, these fish should be heavily stocked to reduce aggression. If there are too few fish, aggression and territoriality may be so fierce that only the strongest or most aggressive fish will survive.

Below: This Labidochromis *sp. is a typical mbuna, or rock-dwelling fish, from the lake. In the aquarium, keep fish such as this in large numbers to reduce the risk of aggression.*

Mouthbrooding

With the exception of one fish, all the cichlid species in the lake are mouthbrooders. Around the barren habitat of the lake there are relatively few places where eggs and young fry can be hidden, so these cichlids have adapted an interesting way to look after their young; they hide them inside their own mouths. After the male has secured a female by various courting displays, they will stay together in an established territory in preparation for spawning. The actual fertilization of eggs, depending on species, often occurs inside the female's mouth and the eggs are not released until they are hatched. The female will first ingest the male's sperm and hold it inside her mouth. She then lays her eggs and picks them up immediately before ingesting

*Right: This female fish (*Melanochromis joanjohnsonae*) is keeping a close eye on her young fry. At any sign of danger she will collect the fry in her mouth, where they will be safe from harm.*

another batch of sperm from the male. This method of fertilization ensures that the maximum number of eggs are fertilized and that predators have little chance to 'steal' any of the eggs. While the eggs develop and hatch inside her mouth, which will take at least 10 days and often up to a month, the female will not feed. Males have little interest in looking after the young, as there are many more females to spawn with. While the young fry grow large enough to cope by themselves, they are dependent on their mother for protection against predators. At the first sign of trouble, the young will gather inside her mouth. Outside, they remain in a close-knit group and never stray far from their mother.

Right: The down-turned mouth of the dolphin cichlid (Pseudotropheus tursiops) *allows it to reach algae in cracks that other fish may not be able to reach. The stunning blue coloration is typical of Lake Malawi fish.*

A DARKENED CAVE

Deep underground is a hidden world where fish survive, sometimes in total darkness. Underwater cave habitats appear in few, often isolated locations around the world, and in this harsh environment nature is tested to its limits.

Conditions in the underwater caves are dark and hostile, and food is hard to find. In caves connected to larger ecosystems, shafts of light may penetrate the dark waters through openings in the cave roof. This light allows plants and algae to grow in isolated spots.

Inside world

Some underwater caves are connected to rivers and lakes, while others are completely cut off from any other aquatic environment.

Cave formation

Caves are usually formed either by erosion or lava flows. Erosion can occur externally, as water from rivers and rain destroy softer rock, while the harder rock above remains intact.

The same type of erosion can occur internally, from rainwater percolating through the rock. Lava flows can occur in geologically active sites, leaving behind a vast network of caves and tunnels. As the lava flow moves across the land, the top surface cools rapidly from the surrounding air and turns into rock.

Underneath, the flow continues and empties to create the caves.

Nothing to see here

Most of the cave habitats that support fish are connected to rivers or streams. Those that are not connected are often only partially underground. Deep into the cave, light can disappear altogether, making sight a relatively useless sense, so many cave fish have either no eyes or very small eyes. Because the fish cannot see, coloration also becomes unimportant; many cave fish have no pigmentation and appear a fleshy colour. In these murky conditions, fish have to use other senses to detect food and move freely within their environment. Sense of smell is generally increased in cave-dwelling fish, helping with both food location and breeding.

Without being able to see a mate, many species will send out chemical signals to identify themselves as ready to breed. The fishes' lateral line system is also used to a great extent in the cave environment. It helps them to locate the walls and floor of their underground home, as well as any obstacles or other fish.

So where is the food?

Virtually all ecosystems rely on sunlight and vegetation as the start of the food chain. In a cave devoid of light there can be no plant matter, so

Below: Some cave environments are completely devoid of light, making eyesight an unnecessary function. Over many years in darkness, fish such as the blind cave fish (Astyanax fasciatus mexicanus) *have lost their eyes and rely on other senses to feed and survive.*

Use a dark substrate for the aquarium floor.

chosen a silver sand base covered with a layer of black gravel. The silver sand is an ideal support for the rockwork and the black gravel adds to the dark cave effect. Alternatively, you could complete the cave using rocks as the substrate. Take care, however, as heavy rocks could crack the tank. It is also possible to obtain coloured sands; in this case, black sand would be an ideal substrate.

here the food chain may begin with bacteria and other microorganisms that feed off sources other than sunlight. Most commonly, the start of life is through sulphur, used by some microorganisms as a source of food. These organisms in turn provide nourishment for the cave's aquatic inhabitants. In caves that are part of a wider, sunlit ecosystem, food can come from various sources, including algae and vegetation.

A safe retreat

Caves that are part of a wider aquatic ecosystem offer protection and hiding places for fish and other inhabitants. In this case, the cave may be used simply as a safe retreat, because the fish can easily leave the cave in search of food or to breed.

The substrate

There are a few options available for the substrate in this setup. Here, we have

Rockwork

You can use any type of inert rock for this setup, providing it is a darkish colour, but the lava rock

Lava rock is ideal for the wall and roof of the cave. Its porous nature makes it light and easy to break into pieces. Use it to create interesting shadows and areas of darkness in the tank.

Cryptocoryne sp. are ideal small plants for this display.

used here is by far the easiest to work with. Lava rock is very porous and light, which means it will place far less pressure on the aquarium floor and is less likely to cause damage in the event of collapse. Due to its porous nature, it is also very brittle and easy to chip and shape, which makes construction easier.

To create the rockwork wall and overhang, silicone pieces of rock in place, either to each other or to the aquarium itself. Fixing the rocks in place will prevent collapse and create a much more secure display. For ease of maintenance, you can silicone the rockwork in sections so that it is easy to remove. In this setup, you should try to use the rocks to stop as much light as possible from entering the aquarium. We have left two areas uncovered in this tank so that light can enter. These shafts of light create an attractive light/dark contrast in the finished display.

Planting

Where shafts of light enter the tank, you can use plants sparingly. An interesting effect can be achieved by planting in the rockwork itself. Lava rock is ideal for this purpose, as plants can root in the many holes and pores. Even so, plants in the rock will need some kind of planting medium to thrive. Fill cracks in the rock either with substrate or with a suitable mineral wool planting medium.

To achieve the desired effect, the rock plants should be short and compact. *Cryptocoryne* sp., as used here, are ideal. On the aquarium floor we have used *Vallisneria americana*, mainly because it will not grow too tall and its light green leaves capture the light well.

Vallisneria americana will rarely grow taller than 20cm (8in) in the aquarium.

Suitable fish

True cave-dwelling fish may be quite hard to get hold of at aquatic dealers, but a few of the available species are found in caves, as well as in other habitats around the world. Some of these fish may not exhibit the exact characteristics of their cave-dwelling counterparts, but they are, nevertheless, the same species.

Blind cave fish

The blind cave fish *(Astyanax fasciatus mexicanus)* must be the most widely known and available cave fish. This small, hardy and undemanding characin will make an excellent addition to a cave aquarium. It has no eyes and detects food by smell, feeding as easily as any sighted fish. The blind cave fish

The darkened cave aquarium

Overhanging walls of lava rock create a dark, brooding atmosphere.

A bed of sand provides support for the rockwork and a covering of darker substrate creates the right atmosphere for this display.

is also quite easy to breed in the aquarium given the right conditions. As young fry, the fish do have eyes and vision, but the eyes are lost as the fry grow older.

Swamp eels
An interesting cave dweller is *Synbranchus infernalis*. This fish is part of the swamp eel group

(Synbranchidae family) of fishes. They are not true eels but certainly look like them, due to their almost total lack of dorsal and anal fins. They are able to breathe air by gulping at the surface. The air is then held in the gills or passed through the gut, where oxygen can be absorbed. If conditions in the cave become poor, the fish can migrate

Place small plants, such as these cryptocorynes, in suitable crevices in the rockwork. Here there are two 'openings' in the cave roof where plants will receive the most light.

The lighting in the aquarium draws attention to the rockface and the plants.

Position smaller pieces of lava rock on the aquarium floor to imitate rocks that have fallen from the cave wall.

Finding food in the cave environment

In dark caves, food is still available from a variety of sources. Sulphur from rocks and springs allow bacteria to grow, on which small animals and shrimps may feed. Many cave fish share their homes with terrestrial animals such as bats that provide nutrients in droppings, and insects, which are a staple diet of many fish. Isolated environments such as these are just one example of the evolutionary success of the fishes, which have adapted to survive in virtually every watery habitat.

Above: *A shoal of blind cave fish (*Astyanax fasciatus mexicanus*) will create a worthy display on their own. These unusual eyeless fish are fascinating to watch; they are every bit as aware of their environment as fully sighted fish.*

Right: Poecilia mexicana *can be found in many caves in nature. In one cave-dwelling population, the fish have developed cave adaptations, although these adapted fish are highly unlikely to be available to fishkeepers.*

over land or bury themselves in mud and hibernate.

Mollies

Although usually found elsewhere, communities of *Poecilia sphenops* and *P. mexicana* do occur in cave environments. In the case of *P. mexicana,* an isolated cave community has adapted to help it survive in this tough environment. The eyes have reduced in size and the sense of smell is greatly increased. These relatively peaceful fish will add a touch of colour to a cave display.

Catfish

To represent the catfish group of fishes, the blind cave-walking catfish *(Clarias cavernicola)* is ideal. This cave-dweller has no eyes or pigment. In the wild it feeds on insects and moths, but in the aquarium it will accept most larger foods. It can grow up to 28cm (11in) in length and will eat smaller fish.

Salamanders

One of the most unusual species available to aquarists is the cave-dwelling salamander, *Proteus anguinus*, also known as the white salamander. In its natural cave habitat it has no eyes and no pigment, but when raised in daylight, eyes develop and the skin becomes a brownish colour. This species is said to live for over 100 years and survive for several years without food. In the cave environment, the salamander uses weak electrical fields to navigate, communicate and locate prey. Although this species of salamander may not be available, many other salamander species are natural cave dwellers.

A BRACKISH ESTUARY

Eventually, every river will reach its final destination – the sea. Salty ocean water mixes with the fresh water of the river and this saline habitat supports many unusual species of fish, all perfectly adapted to otherwise hostile conditions.

There are several kinds of brackish water habitats and some are vast. The fresh water from large rivers entering the sea can dilute the surrounding area over great distances. In other situations, salt water from the sea floods or percolates into freshwater lakes or lagoons.

Chalk and cheese

The mixing of fresh and salt water is a gradual process that creates a whole range of varying salinities. Salt water is much denser than fresh

On the beach

Where the river reaches the sea, it drops silt and sediment, creating sand banks that rise above the water surface and spread over a wide area.

water, so the most saline conditions are always found towards the bottom of the river. For the same reason, the top layer of water will stay fresh further towards the sea. This layering allows many bottom-dwelling marine fish and invertebrates to move up into the river, while the surface-dwellers are held back. In larger rivers, this mixing process will continue for hundreds of kilometres upstream, as well as out into the sea.

Seasonal variations
The brackish area of a river is very loosely defined and will vary daily, seasonally and with changing climatic conditions. Daily variations occur with the rise and fall of the tides. A rising tide will push salt water upstream; when the tide drops, fresh water will come further downstream. Some fish and animals move with this daily variation, sticking to water of the same salinity, while others adjust to the changes.

Seasonal shifts in salinity occur as a result of the amount of water flowing into the sea. When the river is at its highest, full with floodwater from the rainy season, the brackish area is pushed towards the sea. In the dry season, the sea water travels upstream. In rivers such as the Amazon, this seasonal shift can move brackish areas up and downstream by over 200 kilometres (125 miles).

The muck of life
By the time a river reaches the sea, it is carrying a high organic load. Fertile sediment, rich with organic matter, is deposited by the river and provides the ideal conditions for a thriving community of fish and animals. The rich sediment is broken down by numerous bacteria, fungi and microorganisms that are in turn eaten by shrimps and fish. Many molluscs, worms and crustaceans are also found in brackish waters, as well as other filter feeders, all providing an abundant source of food for the fish communities.

Fish – one, plants – nil
Many brackish fish can tolerate a wide range of conditions; some, such as the sailfin molly *(Poecilia latipinna)*, are quite happy either in completely fresh or completely marine conditions. Unfortunately,

Below: The halfbeak (Dermogenys pusillus) *is a small predator found in many brackish waters. Its extended jaw is ideal for catching and crushing its prey.*

plants are not so tolerant of changing conditions and very few aquatic plants grow in brackish conditions. This makes the underwater habitat in the wild quite barren and devoid of vegetation. The lack of plants, combined with constant water flow back and forth, explains why estuarine waters are often muddy, with poor visibility. However, these conditions are one aspect of nature that we will not be trying to recreate in the aquarium.

Substrate

A substrate of fine silver sand will be suitable to recreate the sediment-rich, muddy floor of the estuary. To make this substrate a bit more interesting, add varying grades of gravel around the rocks and wood. You may wish to use some coral sand or coral gravel instead of normal pea gravel. Both of these materials help to buffer the pH in the aquarium and stabilize the water conditions.

Rockwork

As this aquarium is partly marine, You can use any type of rock without any worries about altering water conditions. We have used Westmorland rock to keep the yellow-brown tone of the aquarium.

Westmorland rock has a sandy colour and texture that matches the substrate. In the aquarium it creates an interesting background for fish and plants.

Wood

The wood here is specially processed for aquarium use. It is smooth and a lighter shade than normal aquarium bogwood. We have used quite large, chunky pieces, but smaller ones would work just as well.

Plants

In a naturally brackish habitat, there would be very few, if any, plants. However, the salinity level will be much more stable in the aquarium, so you could add plants for extra interest. Although this may not be entirely true to nature, bear in mind that the aim is to create a display that is suited both to the inhabitants of the tank and to the viewer. In the

This pre-cleaned bogwood has an attractive, twisted appearance.

Most fish dislike the taste of Java fern (Microsorium pteropus), *so it is ideal in this display where many brackish fish will destroy vegetation.*

with plants in a brackish aquarium. The first is that many of the available brackish water fish, such as some of the cichlids, monos and scats, are likely to destroy or eat any vegetation (except Java fern). The second and most important consideration is that plants can also be shocked by sudden changes in water conditions. Any plants intended for a brackish aquarium must be acclimatized slowly to the higher salinity levels.

Additional notes

Most brackish habitats are quite barren and devoid of natural decor, so this aquarium is not entirely true to nature. Nevertheless, it is a much more interesting display than a true

case of this aquascape, adding some vegetation would benefit both. Given the water conditions, relatively few plants will survive and grow in this aquarium. Hardy plants that tolerate brackish conditions include species of *Microsorium, Vallisneria, Anubias, Hygrophila, Sagittaria*, and *Elodea*. The hardiest plants by far are *Vallisneria* sp. and the trusty Java fern *(Microsorium pteropus).* There are two other factors to consider

Once acclimatized, plants such as Vallisneria sp. *will tolerate brackish conditions.*

representation of the natural habitat. Remember that the water conditions in this aquarium are unique. The water should have a salt content of between 10 and 25ppt (parts per thousand). A concentration of 1ppt is equivalent to one gram of salt in one litre of water. Normal seawater has a salt content of 35ppt. Any water added to the aquarium should be ready mixed. You can measure the salinity using a hydrometer. Only use salt specifically designed for aquariums, as table salt will not create the necessary conditions.

Brackish fish

There are many fish available that are naturally found in brackish habitats. Some of these are amongst

The brackish estuary aquarium

The stable salinity levels which can be achieved in the aquarium allow us to use a variety of hardy plants.

The wood in this aquarium represents driftwood from either the ocean shore or the river.

Small pebbles or large pea gravel spread across the sandy substrate creates a more interesting aquarium floor.

the most beautiful fish in the hobby. In addition to many brackish-only species, a number of freshwater species will also do well in brackish waters. Conversely, many brackish species can be acclimatized to freshwater or marine aquariums. Because water conditions and salinity levels in many brackish estuaries are constantly fluctuating, brackish fish have had to adapt to these changing conditions and this makes some species ideally suited to aquarium conditions. Fishkeepers often shy away from keeping brackish fish, considering them difficult and limited in availability. But if you would like to try something a little different but no more difficult, a brackish aquarium is an ideal prospect.

Both Microsorium *and* Anubias *sp. (shown here) will root and proliferate across the wood and rocks.*

The colour and texture of these rocks combine well with the wood and substrate to create an attractive scene.

Take your time

When stocking the aquarium, allow time for the fish to acclimatize to the brackish conditions. Some brackish fish may have been kept in freshwater conditions by the retailer, in which case they should be allowed to settle down in a freshwater aquarium. Once settled, raise the salinity of the water by water changes over a period of weeks. If the fish are already acclimatized to brackish conditions, check the exact salinity using a hydrometer to ensure that there are no major differences when they transfer to your aquarium.

An old favourite

One of the most popular and readily available groups of fish in the hobby are the mollies (Poecilia sp.). Most beginner aquariums house one or more species of molly. All the mollies can be adapted to brackish

Above: The sailfin molly (Poecilia velifera) *is a well known fish. The male (above) sports a fantastic dorsal fin that is actively displayed in the aquarium.*

water and will positively benefit from the addition of salt. In fact, some mollies are prone to health problems if they are kept in purely freshwater aquariums. The sailfin molly *(Poecilia velifera)* can even be acclimatized to purely marine conditions with no ill-effects. Another interesting livebearer is the halfbeak *(Dermogenys pusillus)*. This unusual fish has an extended lower jaw that is connected to the skull. The fish is a predator but will not grow to more than 7.5cm (3in).

Pufferfish

A number of pufferfish are available for the brackish aquarium. They are so-called because they are able to inflate their bodies to almost double their normal size when threatened. The pufferfish have a powerful mouth and strong teeth with which to crush crustaceans to obtain food. In the aquarium, give these fish foods such as cockles so that they can use their teeth as nature intended. If given an incorrect diet, the teeth may become enlarged and cause problems for the fish.

Pufferfish vary a great deal in size, so check to see how big they will grow before introducing them to a community aquarium.

Scats and monos

The monos *(Monodactylis* sp.*)* and scats *(Scatophagus* sp.*)* are the most commonly available purely brackish species. These fish are hardy and adaptable, but will happily destroy many aquarium plants, because vegetation plays a substantial part in their natural diet.

Keep monos and scats in groups; in small numbers they can become aggressive towards each other, which often results in the death of weaker fishes. When young, the scats are beautifully coloured, but they tend to lose colour with age.

And the rest

Many other suitable fish also deserve a mention. However, they may not all be ideal companions in the aquarium, so take care to select those that will live peacefully together. A couple of favourites include the archerfish *(Toxotes jaculator)* and the mudskipper *(Periophthalmus barbarus)* which are discussed in the mangrove biotope (see pages 128-135). Other fish to consider are the bumblebee goby *(Brachygobius doriae)*, mosquito fish *(Gambusia affinis)*, Indian glassfish *(Chanda ranga)*, shark catfish *(Arius seemanni)*, orange chromide *(Etroplus maculatus)*, four-eyes *(Anableps anableps)* and some killifish and rainbowfish.

Below: The scat (Scatophagus argus) *is usually peaceful, but in small numbers a dominant fish will terrorize tankmates.*

A MANGROVE SWAMP

In the brackish areas of larger rivers lie the mangrove swamps. This habitat is unique, but easy to recreate in the aquarium. Many inhabitants of this biotope have unusual behaviours that are a constant source of fascination.

Underwater forest

Beneath the surface, a mass of roots provide hiding places for fishes and other animals. These plants are host and provider to a whole ecosystem.

There are a number of species of mangrove tree, but these are only part of the vegetation that combines to form the mangrove swamps. Mangroves have developed various strategies to cope with the saline water conditions. Some species 'filter out' salt before it enters the roots, sometimes removing more than 90% of it. Others have leaves with special glands that excrete salt. Finally, some mangroves will concentrate and 'collect' salt in bark or old leaves that will drop off, taking the salt with them. To reduce water loss, the leaves of many plants are covered by fine hairs or a thick, waxy coating.

Root overload
The muddy substrate in which the mangrove roots itself is constantly moving and highly unstable. To keep themselves firmly upright and in place, the mangroves produce many

Right: Under the water surface, the mangrove's roots plunge deep into the fertile substrate, branching out for extra stability.

Below: Mudskippers can be found on the nutrient-rich muddy banks of the mangrove swamp, resting and searching for food.

roots. Not far beneath the ground, this muddy substrate becomes stagnant and low in oxygen. Because a low-oxygen environment is not ideal for roots, considerable root growth also takes place above the substrate and smaller roots branch off from the main roots to collect nutrients. The mass of roots thus created make a superb habitat for fish, providing both hiding places and feeding sites.

Providers of food
Mangrove swamps are highly productive habitats. Waste from the mangroves in the form of fruits, leaves and wood is broken down rapidly under the water, providing food for a number of aquatic inhabitants. Bacteria and fungi break down the waste, which can then be eaten by some fish. More waste and debris is taken up by crustaceans and molluscs, which may also become food for fish. Most inhabitants of mangrove areas depend directly or indirectly on the vegetation for their food sources.

The mass of roots from the mangroves also trap any debris that may have been carried downstream by the river systems. This trapped debris provides yet more nutrients that are processed by various organisms and help to sustain the vast mangrove ecosystem.

The substrate
In this aquarium we have used silver sand as a substrate, but fine, lime-free gravel is an alternative. If you wish to keep mudskippers or crabs, you will need to provide an area

above water for them. Here, the sandy substrate is simply piled up towards one end. In a permanent display this will cause big problems. If sand is piled up for any length of time, it will compact, stagnate and eventually produce toxic gases. The best way to prevent stagnation without regularly changing the sand is to adapt a method usually used for plant growth – heating cables. A small, low-wattage heating cable evenly distributed inside the raised area will help to circulate water through the substrate, thus replenishing oxygen and avoiding stagnation.

Another problem with raising the level of the substrate is that in time it is likely to collapse from the constant attentions of the tank inhabitants. This risk can be reduced by using rocks and/or wood to hold the slope in place. However, even with this support, you may find that substrate will need to be regularly replaced.

These rounded slate stones are a good contrast to the sand and can help to maintain the raised substrate.

Twigs and small branches recreate the roots of the mangroves.

Wood

The wood used in this aquarium consists mainly of dead twigs from trees and bushes. These are the best representation of the dense thickets of mangrove roots in the natural habitat. When using wood such as this, it is important to make sure that it is completely dead and dried right through. If it snaps easily without much bending and there is no green coloration inside, then it is probably safe. Check all the twigs carefully to make sure that no vegetation, buds or inhabiting creatures are clinging to them. This wood is very thin – no bigger than 1cm (0.4in) –

and this also helps to ensure that the wood is completely dead and desiccated. Even with these precautions, wood may begin to rot in time. There are two ways to overcome this. The easiest method is simply to replace the wood every few months. For a more permanent display, coat the wood with a suitable and safe varnish.

Giant hygrophila (Hygrophila corymbosa) *will tolerate brackish water.*

Rocks

Rocks are not a vital component of this display, but can be used for extra interest. For both aesthetic and practical reasons, they are best arranged protruding from the sandy hill. The raised substrate is most likely to be quickly eroded near the water surface. Rocks used here will slow the erosion processes and hold the substrate in place.

Plants

If you are able to obtain any of the mangrove species, then they may well grow inside the aquarium, although their success depends on the individual species and complex environmental parameters. We have used giant hygrophila *(Hygrophila corymbosa)*, which has a leaf shape close to that of some mangrove species. This plant is tough and highly adaptable and should survive well in brackish conditions providing it is acclimatized correctly. Remember that the roots are the main feature in this display, so choose plants that will complement and not hide the root structures.

When the tide is out...

It is worth creating a mangrove aquarium simply to keep the wonderful mudskipper (Periophthalmus family). In their natural mangrove habitat, these unusual fish can be found both in and out of the water. When the tide goes out, many small pools and puddles are left on the muddy banks and this is where large groups of mudskippers can be found searching for food in an almost playful manner. As a result of the high organic load of the mangrove swamps, there are countless sources of food available in the mud, and once the tide is out this food becomes easily accessible to the mudskippers. They have adapted in a number of ways to survive out of water. Their skin is covered in liquid-filled cells that reduce the pressures of atmospheric air and stop the skin from drying out. Depressions within the mouth and gill cavities are kept moist and contain many blood vessels for oxygen transfer, allowing the fish to breathe out of water.

Ready... aim...

The archerfish (Toxotes sp.) have developed an amazing way of sourcing food. By firing jets of water at overhanging vegetation, they aim to hit small insects, which fall into the water and become food for the fish. The fish is capable of firing jets of water up to 150cm (60in) above the surface. Archerfish are found in

The mangrove swamp aquarium

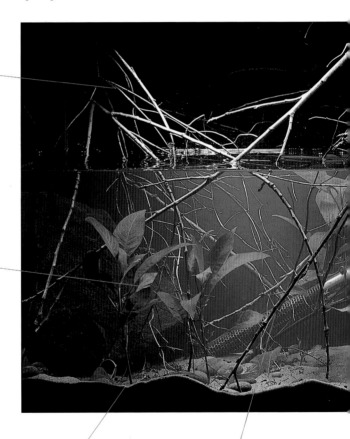

These branches come down from the top of the aquarium, as if they were roots from a tree above the surface.

The Hygrophila *sp. used here looks similar to the leaves of some mangrove species.*

A substrate of silver sand is similar to the natural substrate of the mangrove swamps.

Coat these twigs with a polyurethane varnish or replace them every few weeks.

many brackish areas, including mangroves. In this aquarium, the twigs and roots above water represent the overhanging branches that the archerfish may aim at. If your aquarium has a closed hood, you could introduce insects and flies for the fish to aim at. It is certainly worth trying this because it is truly fascinating to watch the fish at work.

Eye eye
Members of the four-eyes family of fish (Anablepidae) are also surface-dwellers. Their eyes allow them to see both in and out of the water. The eye is divided by a strip of tissue, so that the top half sees above water and the bottom half below. This adaptation helps them to spot any foods on the surface.

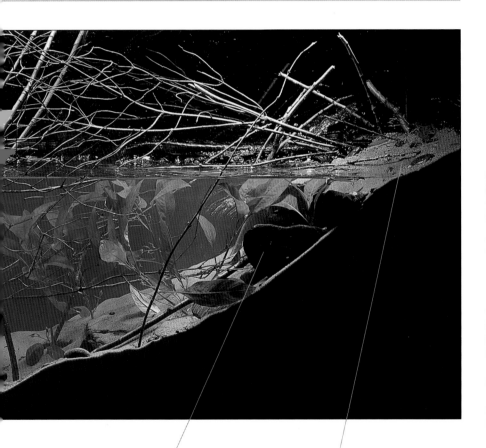

Rocks have been used here to hold the sand in place

This raised area will be home to mudskippers and crabs, which will venture out of the water.

Fiddler crabs

To add more interest to the aquarium, you could add some fiddler crabs. These scavengers will search the tank for debris and waste food. Although they are scavengers, the crabs can cause damage to fish. This is especially the case with male crabs, which have a large front claw used for claiming territories. To avoid this, make sure the tank is not heavily stocked and be careful in your choice of fish. Fiddler crabs are good tankmates for mudskippers and surface dwellers and, like them, appreciate a land area on which to roam about.

Below: The archerfish (Toxotes jaculator) *knocks insects from overhanging branches into the water by firing accurate jets of water. The large angular mouth, flat back and highly developed muscle structure all help this fish to hunt its prey.*

Below: The male fiddler crab (Uca pugnax) *has a single, massively enlarged claw that is used purely for display. These small crabs (2.5cm/1in)) spend their time burrowing in the sand searching for food.*

*Above: The mudskipper (*Periophthalmus barbarus*) is quite happy living out of the water for long periods. In the aquarium, mudskippers can become trusting and confident towards their owner's hand.*

Below: The common name of Anableps anableps *is four-eyes and comes from the fish's ability to see both above and below the water surface, helping the fish to hunt its insect prey more effectively.*

INDEX

Page numbers in **bold** indicate major entries, *italics* refer to captions and annotations; plain type indicates other text entries.

A

Acanthophthalmus kuhlii (Pangio kuhlii) 103
Acipenser ruthenus 77
sp. 77
Acorus sp. 83
African lake cichlids 26
Algae 12, 13, 16, 41, *47*, 49, 56, 57, 105, 109, *111*, 112, 114
Alternanthera reineckii 83
Amazon sword plant 59, 66, 67, *68*
dwarf 99
Amphilophus labiatus 62
Anablepidae 133
Anableps anableps 127, *135*
Angelfish 86, *89*, 93
altum 86
Anubias nana 37
sp. 35, 37, 59, 90, *90*, *93*, 123, *125*
Aquascaping **24-39**
clay pots 31
decor 30-31
fake 30-31
natural 31
branches 31

cork bark 31
snails shells 31
twigs 31
plastic plants 31
rockscapes 34
sealing 31, *31*
Aquatic plants 17, 23, 28, *35*, 37, 39, 48, 50, 59, 67, 75, 82, 89, 90, *90*, 91, *91*, 98, 122, *122*, 127
alpines 39, *43*, *45*
floating 23, 75, *84*, 87, 91, 131
mosses 39
synthetic *83*, *85*
terrestrial bog plants 39, 42, 43
Archerfish 16, 127, 132, 133, *134*
Arenaria caespitosa 'Aurea' 43, *43*
Arius seemanni 127
Arrowana 81, 83
Astyanax fasciatus mexicanus 113, 116, *118*
Aufwuchs 16, 105, 109
Azolla sp. 91

B

Bacteria 21, 114, 118, 120, 129
Bamboo 96, 98, *98*, *100*
Barbs 46
Barbus conchonius 46, *70*
eugrammus 41, 46
ticto 46, *71*
Belonesox belizanus 53, 55
Betta splendens 102, *102*
Bitterling 73, 75, *78*
Blind cave fish *113*, 116, *118*
Blind cave-walking catfish 119
Brachydanio rerio 46
Brachygobius doriae 127
Botia macracanthus 103
Bulldog catfish *18*

C

Cabomba 50, 99
caroliniana 50
sp. 51, *100*
Carassius auratus 78
Catfish 15, 46, 49, *49*, 54, 62, 67, 85, 87, *87*, 94, 119
Berney's shark cat 67
Farlowella 87, *87*
Otocinclus group 46
pictus 49, 54
redtailed cats 15
shark 67, 127
suckermouth 62
whiptail 46, 47
Caves 32, 35, **112-119**
formation 112
Centrarchidae family 78
Ceratophyllum demersum 75, *75*, 77
Chaetostoma sp. *18*
Chanda ranga 127
Characins 51, 93, 116
Chinese hillstream loach 41
Chlamydogobius eremius 65

Cichlasoma
  meeki 57, 62
  nicaraguense 61, *63*
  nigrofasciatum 62
  octofasciatum 61, *62*
  salvini 62
  spilurum 62
Cichlids 93, 105, 123
  Central American 51,
    56, 57, *57*, 58, 59,
    60, 61, 62, 63
  blue-flecked 62
  convict 62
  firemouth *57*, 62
  Jack Dempsey 61, *62*
  Jaguar 61
  Nicaragua 61, *63*
  Quetzal 61
  rainbow 62
  red devil 62
  Lake Malawi *57*, 63,
    104, 107, 108, 109
  dolphin *111*
  'haps' 110
  'mbuna' 110, *110*
Clarias cavenicola 119
Colisa lalia 97, 101
Colossoma sp. 83
Corydoras sp. 94
Crabs 129, 133
  fiddler 134, *134*
Creeping Jenny 75
Cryptocoryne sp. 38, 67,
  67, *68*, *82*, 99, 115,
  115, *117*

D

Danio family 13
Danios 46
Daphnia 12, 41
Dermogenys pusillus
  121, 126
Discus 86, 89, 92, 93, *95*
Dracaena sp. 83
Dragon plant 83
Dwarf otocinclus *47*

E

Echinodorus sp. *53*, 59,
  66, *67*, *68*, *85*, 99
Egeria sp. 38, 75
Eichhornia crassipes 83
Eleotrididae family 68
Elodea
  canadensis 75, 76
  sp. 38, 75, 123
Equipment 20, 21, 22,
  107
  aquarium styles 20, 21
  cabinets 20
  gravel tidy 58
  heater/thermostats 21,
    22, *22*, 29, 31, 50, 60,
    107
  cable *27*, 28
  guard 22, 28, *59*, 60,
    60-61, 107
  hoods 20, *23*
  lighting 21, 22, *117*
    fluorescent tube 22, *23*
    mercury vapour lamp
      23, *23*
    metal halide lamp 23
    spotlights 23
    suspended 39
    underwater 23
  pump 42, 44, 45
    powerhead 43
    sponge 45
Estuaries 19
  brackish 19, **120-127**
  tropical 16
Etroplus maculatus 127

F

Fertilizer 38
Filtration 21, 59, 107
  filters 20, 21, 30, 38
    external power 21, *21*,
      22, 107

inlet pipes 30
  internal power 21, 22
  media *21*
  undergravel 21, 22, 27,
    38
Fish 18, 19, 20, 21, 22,
  23, 25, 26, 29, 35, *35*,
  39, 40, 45, 46, 50, 51,
  53, 56, 57, 64, 65, 67,
  68, 72, 73, 75, 80, 81,
  83, 86, 91, 96, 97, 98,
  99, 100, 104, 105,
  108, 109, 112, 113,
  114, 116, 117, 118,
  119, 120, 121, *122*,
  123, 124
  adding to the aquarium
    16, 17, 18
  algae-eating 31
  breeding 16, 17, 20, 54,
    57, 58, 73, 110-111
  destructive 38
  food 41
    algae 41
    infusoria 41
    mosses 41
    water fleas (daphnia)
      41
  plant-eating 38
Fontinalis antipyretica 75
Forest pool *19*
Fountain plant 83
Four-eyes 127, 133, *135*

G

Gambusia affinis 49, *54*,
  70, 127
Gasteropelecidae family
  87
Gasterosteidae family 73,
  78
Gasterosteus aculeatus
  73
Gobio gobio 70, 76

Goby 67
  bumblebee 127
  desert 65, 67
Goldfish 70
  common 78
Gouramis 20, 101, *103*
  dwarf *97*, 101
  gold 101
  lace *103*
  pearl 101, *103*
Green cabomba 50
Gudgeon 68, 70, 76
Guppy 49, 52, *54*, 70
Gymnocorymbus ternetzi
  85, *86*

H

Halfbeak *121*, 126
Hatchetfishes 87
Hemmigrammus bleheri
  85, *86*
Herotilapia multispinosa
  62
Heteranthera sp. 101
  zosterifolia 82, 90, *93*,
  98, 99, *99*
Hexanematichthys
  graeffei 67
Hoplosternum sp. 94
  thoracatum 94
Hornwort 75, *75*, 77
Houseplants *44-45*
Hydrocotyle sp. *100*
Hygrophila corymbosa 38,
  131, *131*
  giant 131, *131*
  sp. *51*, *52*, 83, 90, *91*,
  92, 123, *132*

I

Indian glassfish 127

J

Japanese rush 83
Java fern 35, 36, *36*, 37,
  38, 59, *59*, 60, 123,
  123
Java moss 36, 37, 43, *44*,
  52

K

Killifish 17, 127

L

Labyrinth fish 17, 96,
  100, 101, 102, *102*
Labidochromis sp. *110*
Lagoons 120
Lake 16, 112
  freshwater 120
  Malawi 11, **104-111**
Lemna sp. 75
Lepomis gibbosus 78, *79*
Livebearers 48, 51, 52,
  55, 126
  breeding *54*
  pike 53
Loaches 17, 47, 102
  Chinese hillstream 47
  clown *103*
  kuhlii *103*
  weather 76
Lobelia cardinalis 98, *99*,
  100
Loricariidae family 62
Ludwigia repens 99
Lysimachia nummularia
  75

M

Malawi cichlids 16
Melanochromis
  joanjohnsonae 110

Mangrove swamps 16, *17*,
  128-135
Melanotaenia
  bosemani 70
  fluviatilis 69
  splendida 69
  trifasciata 65, 69
Microsorium pteropus 35,
  36, 38, 69, 123, *123*
  'Windelov' 59, *59*
  sp. 38, 123, *125*
Minnow 46, 47, 77, 78,
  79
  mountain 47
  piketop *53*, *55*
Misgurnus fossilis 76
Molly 52, 53, 70, 119,
  126
  sailfin 52, 121, 126, *126*
Monodactylis sp. 127
Monos 123, 127
Mosquitofish 49, *54*, 70,
  127
Mouthbrooding 110-111
Mudskippers 16, 127,
  129, *129*, 131, 132,
  133, 134, *135*
Mussels
  freshwater 74
  swan 74
Myletes sp. 83
Myriophyllum
  mattogrossense 99
  sp. 99

N

Nandopsis
  managuensis 61
  umbriferus 62

O

Ophiopogon sp. 83
Orange chromide 127

Osteoglossum sp. 83
Otocinclus affinis 47

P

Pacus 81, 83
Pangio kuhlii
  (Acanthophthalmus
  kuhlii) 103
Paracheirodon axelrodi 84
Periophthalmus family
  131
Periophthalmus
  barbarus 127, *135*
Phoxinus phoxinus 46,
  47, 77, *79*
Pike 73
Pimelodus pictus 49, *49*,
  54
Piranha 81, 83
Pistia stratiotes 83, 91, *91*,
  92, *101*
Plastic plants 38, 39
Platy 52, 53, 70
Plecostomus 13, 62, 63
Poecilia sp. 70, 126
  latipinna 121
  mexicana 118, *119*
  reticulata 49, 52, *54*
  sphenops 52, 119
  velifera 52, 126, *126*
Polyurethane varnish 30,
  36
Potomageton 106
Proteus anguinus 119
Pseudogastromyzon cheni
  41, 47
Pseudotropheus
  tursiops 111
  zebra 105
Pterophyllum
  altum 86
  scalare 89, 93
Pterygoplichthys sp. *63*
Pufferfish 126, 127
Pumpkinseed 78, *79*

R

Rainbowfish 64, 67, 68,
  69, 127
  banded 65
  bosemani 70
Rapids *14*
Rasboras 96, 102
  harlequin 102, *103*
Rasbora heteromorpha
  102, *103*
Rhodeus sericeus amarus
  73, 75, *78*
Riccia sp. 91
River(s) 14, *14*, 15, *15*,
  16, 56, 64, 65, 72, 103,
  112, 113, 120, 128
  Amazon 11, 14, *14*, 80,
  121
  Murry 65
  Negro *14*
Rocks (rockwork) 12, 18,
  19, 22, 23, 24, 32, *32*,
  33, 34, *34*, 35, *35*, *36*,
  37, *37*, 39, 42, *43*, *44*,
  45, *47*, 50, 58, 66, 74,
  98, 105, 106, *106*, 107,
  108, *109*, 112, 114,
  115, *116*, *117*, 122,
  125, 130, 131, *133*
  basalt 28
  bedrock 13
  boulders 13, 76
  calcareous 50, 56
  chalk 28
  coal 28
  cobbles 28, 50, 76, 106
  flint 28
  granite 28
  lava 28, 106, 107, 114,
  114, 115, *116*, *117*
  limestone 28, 49, 50, 56
  marble 28
  pebbles 106, *108*, 124
  plants 115
  quartz 28
  sandstone 28

slate 28, 32, *34*, 42, *42*,
  43, *68*, *130*
synthetic 30, *30*
  spray-on 31
tufa 28
Westmorland 122, *122*
Rooting medium 35
Rosy barb 46, 70

S

Sagittaria sp. 67, *67*, *69*,
  83, 99, 123
Salamander 119
  white 119
Salvinia sp. 91
Scatophagus sp. 127, *127*
Scats 123, 127, *127*
Sedum rupestre
  (reflexum) 43, *43*
Serrasalmus sp. 83
Siamese fighting fish 102,
  102
Silicone sealant 31, *31*,
  32, *32*, 44, 107
Silver dollars 81
Stardust ivy 83
Stargrass 99, *99*
Sterlet 77
Sticklebacks 73, 78
  three-spined *73*
Straight vallis 38, 50, *52*
Streams *12*, *13*, *14*, 40,
  44, 46, 48, 56, 72,
  103, 113
  bed 43
  lowland 48
Striped barb *41*, 46
Sturgeon 77
Sturisoma aureum 46
Substrate 24, 25, 26, 27,
  32, 33, 34, 37, 38, 39,
  42, 43, 49, 50, 58,
  66, 74, 76, 81, 89, 97,
  106, 107, *109*, 114,
  114, 115, 122, *122*,

124, 125, 129, 130
types 24, 25
  basalt chips 26
  calcareous gravel 26, 49
  coloured gravel 26
  coral gravel 26, 28, 107
  crushed coal 26, 82
  gravel *25, 33*, 39, 42, 49, *81*, 82, 114
  lime-free gravel 25, 26, 27, 28, 66, 90, 98, 129
  pea gravel 24, 26, 39, 42, 58, 74, 76, 97, *124*
  pebbles *38*, 39
  sand 25, 26, 27, 28, *35*, 38, *124*
    coral 26, *26*, 49, 107
    silver 25, *33*, 42, 66, 74, 81, *85*, 89, 97, 98, *106*, 114, 122, 129, *132*
  planting 27, *45*, *81*, 82
Sunfish 78
Swamp eels (Synbranchidae family) 117
Swordtail 53, *55*, 70
Symphysodon sp. 86, 92, 95
Synbranchus infernalis 117
Syngonium podophyllum 83
Synthetic tank decorations *30*

T
Tanichthys albonubes 40, 47
Tetras 16, 20, 51, 80, 84, 85, 93, 94

black widow 85, *86*
cardinal 84, 85
neon 85
rummy-nose
  Copyright page, 85, 86
Theraps synspilus 61
Toxotes sp. 132
  jaculator 127, 134
Trichogaster
  leeri 101, *103*
  trichopterus 101
Tropical freshwater fish 11, 12, 16, *102*
Tropical rainforest *13*
Two-spot barb 46

U
Uca pugnax 134

V
Vallisneria sp. 38, 106, 123, *123*
  aethiopica 106
  americana 115
  spiralis 38, 50, 51, *52*
Vesicularia dubyana 36, 52

W
Water
  acid 17, 18, 24, 28, 29
  alkaline 18, 24, 28, 41, 50, 51, 52, 56
  brackish 15, 16, *17*, 38, 65, 126, 127, 128, 131, 133
  fish 16
  chemistry 24, 25, 26, 28, 30
  hard(ness) 24, 26, 28, 38, 41, 51, 52, 107

oxygen level 30, 38, 41
pH level 16, 24, 26, *26*, 28, 29, 49, 51, 56, 85, 88, 89, 90, 92, 97, 107
quality 14, 28, 51, 85
  in nature *14*
salinity 16, 120, 121, 122, 123, 124, *124*, 125
soft 24
Waterfalls 12, 13, *14*, 32, 41, 45
  feature 42, 43, 44
Water hyacinth 83
Water lettuce 83, 91, *91*, 92, *100*
Whiptail catfish 13
White Cloud Mountain minnow 13, 40, 47
Willow moss 75
Wood 13, *18*, 22, 23, 24, 35, 36, *36*, 37, *37*, 43, 50, 59, 66, *66*, 67, 68, 74, 77, 82, *85*, 90, 98, 122, 124, *125*, 130, 131
  bark 32, *82*, 84
  bogwood *18*, 29, *29*, 30, 32, 33, *35*, 36, 37, *38*, 39, 43, *43*, 44, 52, 59, 74, 82, 90, *90*, 92, 93, *101*, 122, *122*
  'Jati wood' 29
  branches/twigs 19, 36
  driftwood 19, 124
  synthetic 30, *30*, 74, 75

X
Xiphophorus sp. 70
  helleri 53, 55
  maculatus 52

Z
Zebra denio 46

CREDITS

The practical photographs featured in this book have been taken by Geoffrey Rogers and are © Interpet Publishing.

The publishers would like to thank the following photographers for providing images, credited here by page number and position: B(Bottom), T(Top), C(Centre), BL(Bottom left), etc.

Ardea London: 13(P Morris), 17(Jean-Paul Ferrero), 64(Jean-Paul Ferrero), 96(Joanna van Gruisen), 111(B, Liz & Tony Bomford), 120(C, Eric Lindgren), 128(C, Don Hadden), 129(T,C, Ron & Valerie Taylor)
MP & C Piednoir/Aqua Press: Half-title page, copyright page, 10, 12, 19, 54(B), 55(B), 57, 62, 71(B), 118, 126, 134(T), 135(T)
Hans-Georg Evers: 54(T), 56, 63(T), 80, 97, 110, 119, 121
John Feltwell/Wildlife Matters: Title page, 14, 40, 48, 72, 88(Jeremy Hoare)
Photomax (Max Gibbs): 49, 71(T), 79(T,B), 111(C), 135(B)
Planet Earth Pictures: 112(Javier G Corripio)
Mike Sandford: 41, 46, 47, 63(B), 65, 78, 86(T,C), 87, 89(T), 94, 95, 102, 103(C,B), 113, 127, 134(B)
Sue Scott: 104, 105
W A Tomey: 18, 55(T), 70, 73, 129(C)

The artwork illustrations have been prepared by Stuart Watkinson and are © Interpet Publishing.

ACKNOWLEDGMENTS

The publishers would like to thank Jason Scott and all his staff at The Water Zoo, 439 Lincoln Road, Millfield, Peterborough PE1 2PE for their generous help and for providing valuable space to photograph the biotope aquariums featured in this book. Thanks are also due to Swallow Aquatics, London Road, Rayleigh, Essex SS6 9ES and Hobby Fish Farm, Old Stratford, Milton Keynes MK19 6BD.

The information and recommendations in this book are given without any guarantees on the part of the author and publisher, who disclaim any liability with the use of this material.